Pet Food &
Tropical Apparitions

Also by Jessica Hagedorn

Dangerous Music (Momo's Press, 1975)

Jessica Tarahata Hagedorn

Pet Food & Tropical Apparitions

Momo's Press   1981   San Francisco

Pet Food and Tropical Apparitions

Thanks to the Creative Artists Public Service
program of the New York State Council for
the Arts and the Basement Workshop (New
York City) for providing funds and time to
complete this volume.

Acknowledgement and tribute to the
Yardbird Reader, Washington Review of the
Arts, Sojourner, Ark, Greenfield Review,
Third World Women (Third World Communi-
cations), and **Omens from the Flight of Birds:
The First 101 Days of Jimmy Carter** (Momo's
Press), where a number of these works
originally appeared.

Lyrics quoted in "Motown / Smokey
Robinson" are from two songs by
Smokey Robinson, respectively "Tracks of
My Tears" and "You Really Gotta Hold On
Me," © Jobette

Funding for this production was made par-
tially possible by grants from the National
Endowment for the Arts, a Federal Agency,
and the California Arts Council.

Momo's Press
45 Sheridan Street
San Francisco CA 94103

**Library of Congress Cataloging
in Publication Data**

Hagedorn, Jessica Tarahata, 1949–
Pet food and tropical apparitions.

PS3558.A3228P47   813'.54   81-11058
ISBN 0-917672-15-1   AACR2
ISBN 0-917672-14-3 (pbk.)

First printing
Printed in the United States of America

for the twins, my mother
and aunt, Elizabeth & Pearl—
in appreciation of their beauty,
tenacity & strength;
and in memory of Bob Marley—
for his words
and his music

Contents

Pet Food &
Tropical Apparitions

Motown / Smokey Robinson

hey girl, how long you been here?
did you come with yr daddy in 1959 on a second-class boat
cryin' all the while cuz you didn't want to leave the barrio
the girls back there who wore their hair loose
lotsa orange lipstick and movies on sundays
quiapo market in the morning, yr grandma chewin' red tobacco
roast pig? . . . yeah, and it tasted good . . .
hey girl, did you haveta live in stockton with yr daddy
and talk to old farmers who immigrated in 1941?
did yr daddy promise you to a fifty-eight-year-old bachelor
who stank of cigars . . . and did you
run away to san francisco / go to poly high / rat your hair /
hang around woolworth's / chinatown at three in the morning
go to the cow palace and catch SMOKEY ROBINSON
cry and scream at his gold jacket
Dance every friday night in the mission / go steady with ruben?
(yr daddy can't stand it cuz he's a spik.)
and the sailors you dreamed of in manila with yellow hair
did they take you to the beach to ride the ferris wheel?
Life's never been so fine!
you and carmen harmonize "be my baby" by the ronettes
and 1965 you get laid at a party / carmen's house
and you get pregnant and ruben marries you
and you give up harmonizing . . .
hey girl, you sleep without dreams
and remember the barrios and how it's all the same:
manila / the mission / chinatown / east l.a. / harlem / fillmore st.
and you're gettin' kinda fat and smokey robinson's gettin' old

> **so take a good look at my face / you see my smile**
> **looks outta place / if you look closer / it's easy to trace /**
> **the tracks of my tears . . .**

but he still looks good!!!

> **i don't want to / but i need you / seems like i'm always /**
> **thinkin' of you / though you do me wrong now / my love is**
> **strong now / you really gotta hold on me . . .**

Bump City:
A Fairytale for the 20th Century

After a bit of guacamole and chile relleno at the roosevelt tamale parlor ruby and juanita took the bus to market st. and got off by church st. where the reliable safeway was located, its blue lights soft and almost soothing in the winter night. They both decided to get some bubble gum and maybe some pear wine, juanita feeling kinda blue after having lost her man, the sweet fawn who had been kidnapped by the white bandits.

The safeway was crowded with all sorts of folks, in their tweed winter coats and vinyl bandanas, with toni easy-perm rollers in their hair and purple umbrellas and green lizard handbags and black see-through pimp socks. Ruby immediately left juanita and headed for the candy department, and juanita went to the liquor and frozen foods section cuz she was getting kinda hungry again. In the middle of the refrigerated vernor's ginger ale and espanada and swanson teriyaki pies, she ran into soul sister number one, who was trying to decide whether she should get beer or splurge on a small bottle of jack daniels. They fried out on seeing each other and wished a happy new year to themselves and everybody else including ruby, who by this time had a whole shopping cart full of bubble gum and bean dip and laura scudder potato chips.

Soul sister number one almost puked when she saw the shopping cart, maybe cuz she'd never seen anybody so obsessed with bubble gum in all her life. Finally she gave up trying to figure things out and picked a pack of miller's high life beer, while juanita got a bottle of ripple pear wine, and they all three strolled over to the cashier, but of course there were lines of tired and hungry and irritable people in every lane. Being in a good mood by now, the three of them shucked and jived in lane number 6, which was the fast lane, no more than six items or less, please . . . , when who should juanita see but the very manifestation of the archangel lucifer and young king tut himself, no more than eight years old, a baby stud, a real winner, sitting all by himself by the exit, obviously waiting for his mommy or daddy to finish shopping. Well, juanita almost fell over her bottle of ripple in her excitement, and she jabbed ruby's pectoral muscles with her some-what bony elbow.

"Look—i'm in love!" she exclaimed, in a swoon.

She pointed to the child in a most immodest manner. All three stared at the child in amazement, for he was beautiful, with a head full of black curls and kinks like a zulu crown, and skin that was the sleekest brown, eyes that were neither green nor yellow, like some stray puma in the jungle.

Of course he aroused lecherous ideas in juanita, but ruby and soul sister number one dragged her out of safeway before the child could say

BOO, which he was planning to do, having found the three of them very amusing. Juanita moaned and groaned in the true agony of the blues as they pushed her into soul sister's 1959 blue mercury, and they drove off, listening to juanita holler for mercy, and finally ruby opened the bottle of pear wine and jammed it down juanita's throat to shut her up. Juanita calmed down into a stupor after the bottle was about half emptied, and they drove faster down the freeway shucking and jiving to the joe cuba sextet: **wham bang! push n shove—i'll never go back to Georgia / i'll never go back.**

When they finally got to bump city, they were ready.

Bump city's colors are red and purple. The air is smokey and warm, and there's a closet in the back room with enough space for the good folks to pile into and snort up when they feel like it.

Soul sister number one had a gig that night, and all the hangerouters were there from the bizarro–oakland–san francisco family: bizoni the drummer and bizarta his beautiful creole lady, bizola who danced like amazing african cotton candy dreams, bizrol her younger sister, bizezika who was really juanita in unreal life, and a whole mess of drunkards just in from the ozone.

The bizarro family was drinking tequila, and juanita held on to ruby cuz she was feeling wobbly. They all sat together at one table, all on top of one another and all over each other's tits and laps, drunk as a skunk and loose as a goose before the music even started. Fast freddy, who couldn't have been that sly, slithered over to juanita, who by this time was pretty much under the table, and whispered that the white girl was in town.

"You don' mean the waitress!" blithered juanita.

"No man—you know what i mean—" fast freddy said, looking anxious.

Slowly the meaning of his words sunk into juanita's ripple-fogged brain. "Oh yeah?" Her eyes lit up, and so did her nose.

Freddy the fox took her arm and helped her walk to the back room of the nightclub and they found the closet which was jammed with about ten or twenty degenerates, and they had to crawl over all these sweating bodies decked out in gold and silver lamé, hot pink hotpants, chartreuse borsalino hats, pastel ice cream suits, and leopard-skin turbans.

They squeezed in between the folks, and juanita brought out her para-phernalia which she had long ago learned never to be without: her mirror inside a delicate antique compact case, a razor blade, and a plastic straw. Freddy the fox was usually tight with his dope, particularly the good kind—but it seemed that tonight everybody was under the influence of some magic, even slick cocaine dealers. So juanita had herself a high old time in that closet and stumbled out in time for soul sister number one's first song, an old tune by dyke and the blazers, which got everybody even drunker than before. The grease boys pulled out a bottle of pagan pink from under the table, and the bizarro family guzzled it in style, and pretty soon even chepito was yelling "suck my dick," and the grease boys were

13

laughing and pulling up their shirts to show off smooth brown bellies, and juanita was doing the penguin and burning a hole in the floor.

Soul sister number one finished her first set and came back to the table and had some more beer, and pretty soon she broke the bottle on the edge of the table smiling all the while and pointing the jagged head at anyone who came near. Juanita giggled until she almost peed in her pants, and benjy the pimp came over and asked ruby to dance who had been quiet most of the time, and benjy confessed that he really wasn't a shoe sales-man but a pimp that specialized in white girls.

"Oh—you mean cocaine?" blithered ruby.

"No man—" he said, pointing to the waitress, who looked kinda jewish and dyed her hair the color of strawberries and wore a yellow jumpsuit.

"Oh yeah?" ruby said, her eyes lit up in a kind of angry disap-pointment. She went back to the table and ordered more tequila to soothe her temper.

The magic had exploded into anger, with everyone breaking bottles and threatening everyone else in fun and frustration, and juanita was high and oblivious to the energy around her, and she kept dancing and dreaming about young king tut back at the safeway. What was his daddy like? she wondered.

Soul sister number one got back on the bandstand and sang some more, her eyes glazed over: **can i dedicate /** . . . **to you n you n you.**

Bizoni the drummer was pounding away at his drums, and the jewish waitress cleared the tables of broken glass and empty bottles and scattered batangas switchblades, and in the middle of the debris and the music who walked in to blow juanita's mind but young king tut's daddy himself   in person   the real thing   the real winner.

He was decked out in purple robes, and juanita stared at him in drugged shock. Young king tut's daddy was her man. Her soul was taken away at the sight of him. They danced together, wordless, and soul sister finished her last song. Tables were overturned.

In the mad scramble to dance and shimmy and shake bump city went up in flames. Drums floated in the sky.

Fish swam out of the mouths of trumpets.

The moon was cut in half and women bled.

In the early morning the street shimmered with diamond fragments. They staggered out the door quietly laughing, traces of blood still on them.

The Leopard

once undressed
your markings
are displayed
with elegance
the languid dance
before you execute
your prey

as if
i didn't know
i was the kill.
your tongue
camouflaging growls
with a kiss.

in costume
you casually join
the crowd
gaping at museum walls
oohing and aahing
with the best of them.

you slip a hand
into my dress
tenderly fondling
each breast
as if
i didn't know
about those claws
pulled back
inside the fur.

Pet Food

In the distance I could hear the Four Tops singing
Standing in the shadows of love . . .

"My candelabra are missing!!!" Auntie Greta's Mario Lanza shriek pierced the tense silence in the living room of our tiny, overfurnished apartment.

My mother Consuelo rolled her eyes at the familiar sound of Auntie Greta's high-pitched voice. "There he goes again," she muttered to herself, annoyed. She was not speaking to me.

I studied my beautiful mother's face, wanting to touch it. Even in anger she seemed so vulnerable. I liked to think she was vulnerable to me, ever since my entomologist father had run off with the nubile Princess Taratara to the rain forests of Mindanao. They claimed to be on an expedition hunting for prehistoric dragonflies.

We were sitting across from each other in the cluttered living room: my mother Consuelo on the Empress Josephine couch, her frail body lost in the busyness around her. A leopard-skin rug hung on the wall above her head. The rug was one of her prize possessions—a gift from my father when they were still together. I was seated on the ornately carved Spanish colonial chair we had brought on the ship with us when we came from the islands. My mother and I had been sitting like this for more than an hour, and my ass was killing me. I had been trying to explain why it was important for me to move out of her house.

"Dios mio!" she kept moaning. "You'll be the death of me yet!" Her eyes hardened, and her voice suddenly changed from weepy martyr to righteous district attorney. "I know who's responsible for this. It's that so-called 'friend' of yours, Boogie. I warned you about him, but of course you never listen. You're always defending those smelly friends of yours."

"Boogie doesn't **smell**," I retorted. "He wears tangerine oil."

"That boy smells like a fruit, all right," my mother said, smugly. "He's no good—a drug addict with too many crazy ideas. DON'T SMIRK!" she snapped at me. "I wasn't born yesterday, you know. It's all in the eyes, George. I can see the **end** in his eyes. That boy's always hopped up. Pretends he plays the piano. Pretends he plays the guitar. A DISGRACE TO THE RACE, that's what he is. Oh, well," she sighed again, "wasn't he born here anyway?"

"Yeah," I said. "In Stockton. His family covers their couches and lampshades in plastic."

My mother was triumphant. **"I knew it!** That boy's an American-born pinoy with no class. He's going to drag you down with him."

"That's not true," I said. "Boogie's one of the gentlest, most sensitive people I know. He looks out for me."

"Looks out for you??? You think I don't know about your little adventures with that low-life fairy? Always running off to so-called concerts with him, coming home at three in the morning and watching television until seven? He smiles up in my face and says, 'Good evening, Mrs. Sand. Thank you so much for letting George go out with me.' Meanwhile, you come home late and can't sleep at all! **DRUGS!** Drugs and sex—that's all you kids think about! You were all right before you met him," she whined.

We went around in circles, crying and hurling accusations at each other, until Auntie Greta stormed into the apartment, his Chihuahua Revenge on a rhinestone-studded leash. Revenge was quivering and shaking and yapping at everything in sight.

My mother pressed a carefully manicured hand to her forehead. "GRETA, PLEASE—that dog of yours should be put to sleep. **She stinks.** Everytime you drag her in here I have to get down on my hands and knees and shampoo the rug! And her goddam yelping gives me a headache."

I smiled. "Hello, Auntie Greta," I said, pretending my mother wasn't there. "How's your day been?"

Auntie Greta gave my mother a deadly look. "Thank you, dear—it's been perfectly dreadful. My antique Barcelona candelabra are missing."

"One of your boys must've stolen them," my mother suggested sweetly.

Auntie Greta plopped down on a pink brocade Louis Quinze chair and placed the shivering Chihuahua on his lap. "My boys? My dear, how could you say such a thing!"

Auntie Greta, my dear uncle and aunt all in one, was a distant relative on my mother's side of the family. He had been in America for twenty years and worked in San Francisco as a semi-fashionable hairdresser in a stuffy salon that still believed in pincurls. His clients were a small but loyal group of wealthy matrons who liked their hair set, teased, and dyed silver-blue. When my mother left my father and took me to America, leaving behind all the tropicalismé in our lives, she had no choice but to look up Auntie Greta, the only person she knew in San Francisco. Auntie Greta helped raise me by acting as a handy and enthusiastic chaperone, especially when my mother didn't want to be bothered. I was very fond of Auntie Greta—he loved the movies as much as I did and tried unsuccessfully to sneak me into the gay bars he frequented so I could have my first drink with him, "just like a grown-up." He looked at me with some embarrassment while my mother lit a cigarette and ignored me.

"Greta, dear, you know exactly what I'm talking about," she said coolly. "I'm referring to those boys on the street you pick up and bring home—the ones you feed and clothe, who are always beating you up and burglarizing your apartment."

Martha and The Vandellas' **Your Love Is Like a Heat Wave** was churning in my head as I looked away, avoiding Auntie Greta's pained

17

expression. I had to agree—my mother was right. In fact, that was the very reason she had asked Auntie Greta to move out of our apartment—he kept bringing these surly and suspicious youths home, making my mother more paranoid than ever. He finally moved to a studio on the floor directly above us and, except for the times when he was involved in a "hot romance," we saw him everyday at dinnertime.

Auntie Greta's eyes widened in horror. "Oh my god, Consuelo! You don't think that sweet boy Alex could've done it, do you? Not Alex! He's not capable of such an act."

My mother sailed off into the kitchen to make a pot of coffee. "Oh, no?" she called out cheerfully from the kitchen. "Your boy Alex is certainly capable of anything, darling. It's all in his eyes. **I can tell**. Plus he's got a weak chin—that's why he's trying to grow that mangy beard. Who does he think he's kidding? As I was just telling my daughter, George—who never listens to her mother, of course—all these young people are after the same thing these days—drugs and sex, drugs and sex—and they want it all for **free**."

I sat there quietly, listening to my mother putter around the kitchen and trying not to lose my temper. I turned to Auntie Greta. "I'm leaving."

"Leaving? But you haven't had dinner yet," he said, looking concerned.

I shook my head. "I'm leaving **home**—and the sooner the better. That's why she's pissed at me."

"I wondered why she was pretending you were invisible," Auntie Greta said, "but then I've always thought Consuelo was into high drama. I never know what to expect when I come downstairs. She's so moody."

"Well, I'm packed and ready to go."

"Do you have any money?" Auntie Greta asked.

I shrugged. "A little bit I saved from the birthday check Dad sent."

He stared at me with some amazement. "But that's not enough! Where are you going to go? You don't even have a job! Where are you going to live? This is all too sudden, even for me—," Auntie Greta said, getting more upset by the minute. "Dear girl, why don't you stay here a while longer, get yourself a job, then move out? That's the sensible way to do things."

I grinned. "Oh, Auntie Greta. I'll be all right. I have friends. They'll look out for me."

"Look out for you? Who's going to look out for you the way your mother and I look out for you? Consuelo may be temperamental, but she's a tigress who loves you **fiercely**."

I grimaced, but Auntie Greta ranted on. "It gets in the way sometimes, but she cares, she really does!"

"I can't take it," I said, "she's too **intolerant**. And she hates Boogie so much."

Auntie Greta sighed. "She just doesn't understand the American way of life. It's too fast for her. Everything's changing, including you." He paused, studying me carefully. "You're not in trouble, are you?"

I shook my head, still grinning. I was going to miss Auntie Greta

18

very much.

"What about drugs?" he asked. "Consuelo informed me that she found a joint in your bookbag once. I had to give her some of my Valiums to calm her down. Was that true?"

I nodded, remembering how Consuelo had burst into my room the morning after she found it, as I was on my way to school. "Everyone experiments," was all I had said to her, which sent her further into her rage.

"Dear George," Auntie Greta pleaded, "you must be careful about the company you keep. Who am I to tell you this, you're probably thinking . . . but I **know**. Aren't you going to college? Don't you have any plans?" Auntie Greta's desperate tone made me nervous.

"Not really," I replied. "I just want to live on my own for a while. Maybe write a little bit. See what happens."

"See what happens? My dear, you're much too vague—no wonder Consuelo's so upset!" Auntie Greta groaned.

I stared off into space.

He got up from the chair and reached into the pocket of his elegantly tailored gabardine pants. "Here. It isn't much, but it should help," he said, handing me a roll of bills.

I tried to give it back to him, but he ignored my outstretched hand. "Take it, for godsake—I know you'll need it," Auntie Greta said, in a firm tone of voice that was new to me. "Let us know as soon as you get settled. And please—please be careful."

I felt like a son being sent off to an unpopular war as I stood uncertainly in the dim foyer, waiting for my mother to come out of the kitchen so I could say goodbye. She never did.

Maybe she heard everything that was said between Auntie Greta and me and, angry as she was, that was enough for her. She often said that walls have ears.

Telling myself over and over again that I had done the right thing, I sang this as I walked down the street:

Little Richard
Tutti-Frutti
Fats Domino
I'm walkin' . . .
are you ready for a brand new beat?
Summer's here
the time is right
for dancin' in the street . . .
Sal Mineo
James Dean
Marlon Brando
Rat-hole
Rabbit-hole
and Goodbye, Feets!

The sign dangled from the fire escape in front of the shabby building:

STUDIO APT. FOR RENT

I entered the lobby of the dimly lit building, one of those victorian San Francisco dwellings that must've been grand in the early 1900s. Times had certainly changed—the neighborhood had quietly deteriorated and the building had decayed right along with it. It still had marvelous dark wood panelings and art nouveau, daffodil-shaped lamps along the walls, but the carpets were stained and faded, and you could smell the grease emanating from the apartments. Another faded sign in the lobby read:

STANLEY GENDZEL—MANAGER—APT. 1
COLLECTOR OF ANTIQUES—PARROT MAN EXTRAORDINAIRE

I hesitated before knocking on his door. Bells tinkled faintly, and someone came toward me down the dark, dank hallway. I put my suitcase down and whirled around to face the young man who stood there, staring at me. Could this be Stanley Gendzel? I wondered.

Barefoot, the young man held a large orange cat in his arms. The cat gazed at me with the same dispassionate curiosity.

The young man and the cat bore a striking similarity—the young man with copper-colored skin, slender and beautiful, with his ominous lion's-mane hair, the color of brown fading into reddish-gold, much like the extraordinary cat's thick fur. After a few moments, the young man put the cat down, and we both watched it scurry away into the darkness.

"I'm looking for the manager," I said.

The young man smiled. "Manager?"

Oh no, I thought, this couldn't be Stanley Gendzel!

"I'm looking for a place to live," I said, as firmly as I could. Looking for an apartment of my own was one of the momentous decisions of my life, and I was determined to act as adult and businesslike as possible.

"Oh," the young man said, still being playful with me. "A **place**. You need a place."

"I certainly do," I retorted.

"Then you need to see Stanley," he said.

There was a moment of silence, and we looked each other over like two animals sniffing each other out.

Suddenly he said, "Let me show you my guitar."

I shook my head. "No."

"Let me show you my cello."

"No." Where was Stanley Gendzel?

"Let me show you my saxophone."

"No!"

"Let me show you my soprano saxophone."

"Hmmmm. . . ." I was getting curious.

"Let me show you my bass saxophone."

"Oooh. . . ."

20

He was relentless. "Let me show you my bass clarinet."

"Oh dear," I sighed, slowly wearing down.

"Let me show you my bass."

My favorite instrument. I looked him dead in the eye. "Upright or electric?"

He grinned. "Both."

It had been a long day. I decided I must be falling in love, and to hell with Stanley Gendzel. "Well," I said, "maybe . . ."

His grin widened, and suddenly—like magic—the dank and forbidding hallway seemed less gloomy. "My berimbau? Caxixi? Sansa?"

He was so enthusiastic and strangely radiant, I had to give in.

"OKAY!" I responded, smiling back at him and taking his hand.

I followed him up the first flight of stairs, and he pulled out a gleaming gold key and unlocked the door to an apartment. The living room was littered with every kind of musical instrument imaginable, and an orchestra of children was playing. Their faces were painted like ornate African and Balinese masks. Bells hung from the ceiling. We began to dance in slow motion, lost in some kind of trancelike, sensuous waltz.

My first and only lover so far had been Junior Burgess, who could sing as compellingly as Smokey Robinson, seducing me sweetly with his voice while telling me stories of all my favorite Motown groups. But this young man who held me in his arms was different. He **glowed**. He made me so nervous I blurted out "I love you" in the middle of our dance.

His face was devoid of expression, like the cat who sat purring in the room, so sure of its regal beauty. "I know," he said, not unkindly.

"My name is George Sand," I told him shyly.

"I know," the young man said.

"Your name is Rover," I said.

"Exactly," he replied, twirling me around the room. I don't know how much time we spent in that room, the children's orchestra continuously serenading us with their dissonant circus music, the purring orange cat never once taking his amber eyes off our dancing bodies. And I didn't care.

I floated out of Rover's apartment in a daze, starting back down the stairs in my second attempt to locate the mysterious Stanley Gendzel, manager of this illustrious building. I dragged my battered suitcase behind me, unsure of what had just happened. All I remembered was that late afternoon softly changed into darkness, and the children's orchestra stopped playing, and Rover and I stopped dancing, unwinding slowly like two figures twirling on top of a music box. The big orange cat rubbed against our legs, and Rover picked him up and carried him in his arms, stroking his fur gently. He kissed me on my lips, then once—very tenderly—on each of my eyelids. "I will see you again," was all he said.

A darkly beautiful Sephardic Jewish woman came bounding up the stairs as I was on my way back down to Stanley Gendzel's apartment. She seemed to be in her early twenties, dressed in interesting layers of clothing my friend Boogie would've called "fleamarket glamor." Crocheted doilies had been sewn together into a lacey shirt worn over red satin pyjamas. The pyjamas were stuffed into embroidered Nepalese boots. She was carrying a blender in one hand and a large black portfolio in the other.

"Hey," she called out, in a friendly way. "You new in the building? Silver Daddy's new piece of cheese, perhaps?"

"Uh, no."

She peered at me from under the thick fringe of her black eyelashes. "My name is Momma Magenta," she finally said.

"Hi. I'm George."

She never flinched. "You're very much his type, you know. Are you Indian or something? Mexican? Italian, somewhat?"

"No, not any of those," I said wryly.

"What about Japanese? That's Silver Daddy's new trip. THE JAPANESE . . . he's busy editing an anthology of esoteric Japanese poets. 'O Momma Magenta,' he's always telling me, 'you've got all the right ingredients. Long black hair, black eyes, big tits, a small waist, and a big ass . . . but you aren't JAPANESE!' I'm always showing him my portfolio, you know," she chattered confidentially. "After all, Silver Daddy's one of America's oldest living legends, with plenty of connections in the art world. But all he ever wants to do around me is talk about pussy."

"Oh. You're an artist?"

Momma Magenta was obviously pleased that I had asked this question. "Yeah, that's right. I do rock n' roll posters. Wanna see my portfolio?"

"No thanks. I don't have time. I'm looking for a place to rent."

"Well, you've come to the right place, sweetie. Silver Daddy owns this building, see. He's what you might call a bonafide **artiste** and slum landlord all rolled into one. He lives on the top floor, in his fashionable ghetto penthouse. You're in luck. Silver Daddy just ordered Stanley Gendzel to kick one of the tenants out. He was a poet from New York named Paolo. Trouble was, he was a smack freak, and broke all the time. HEY— wanna buy a used blender?"

I started down the stairs. "No thanks, really. I think I should go see about renting this apartment," I said, waving goodbye to her.

"Good luck with Stanley,'" she waved back. "Don't let **him** chew your ears off. And don't be surprised when Silver Daddy invites you up for one of his famous dinner parties."

Something that resembled a shrivelled up spider with bushy eyebrows for antennae opened the door. "Whadda ya want?" he croaked, looking me up and down.

"I'm interested in renting the apartment," I said. "Are you Mr. Gendzel?"

"Yup. I'm Stanley Gendzel. Come in, come in." He stepped aside to let me through the door. I pretended not to notice that all he had on were faded, yellow boxer shorts. A large green parrot was perched on his shoulder.

He ushered me into his grimy kitchen and pulled out a chair for me. For a long while no one said a word. I watched Stanley scratch the bird's head, cooing softly to the creature. Then he pulled out a box of birdseed and nonchalantly placed some seeds on the tip of his tongue. The parrot pecked the food off the old man's outstretched tongue while the old man stared at me suspiciously.

"Are you a college student?" he asked suddenly, when the parrot finished his dinner.

"No, I'm a poet," I blurted out, wondering if I'd said the wrong thing.

Stanley was visibly upset. "A poet! Not another one!"

It had been such a long, grueling day that between my mother and Auntie Greta's hysterics and Momma Magenta's aggressiveness, I decided I just couldn't accept Stanley's disapproval. I had to convince this strange man that I had to have the apartment this very evening. Besides, it was getting late and I was hungry.

"Yes," I said, as calmly and politely as possible. "I'm a very responsible person, in spite of what you might think. How much is the rent?"

"Well," Stanley said, scratching the parrot's head once again, "it's one of the worst studios in the building. That heroin addict never cleaned up after himself. Always sipping grape soda and munching Twinkies! It's a wonder he's still alive. Left behind reams and reams of paper—some with writing on it, some without. I didn't have the heart to destroy his work, even though Silver Daddy didn't think too highly of it. He ordered me to go in there and disinfect everything and burn all the boy's manuscripts. Imagine! I just couldn't do it," Stanley repeated, shaking his head slowly.

"I'm glad you didn't. I'm sure Paolo would appreciate it," I said.

"Humph!" Stanley snorted. "Paolo didn't appreciate anything—that's why he was so self-destructive. Anyway, I haven't cleaned the place at all, so you can have it for eighty dollars a month, no cleaning deposit necessary. The toilet works, and if you wanna paint it, Silver Daddy will insist on raising the rent, so I wouldn't advise it. Just leave well enough alone."

I got up to go. "Thanks very much, Mr. Gendzel."

"What'd you say your name was again?" he asked.

"I didn't. My name is George Sand."

"Interesting name for a young girl. You look very interesting, by the way. You wouldn't happen to be Japanese, would you?"

"No, I'm from the Philippines, actually. My mother brought me here when I was very young," I replied.

He seemed totally disinterested. "Oh. **The Philippines.** All I remember is that big fuss about MacArthur. Well, it doesn't really matter. I'm sure

24

Silver Daddy will invite you to dinner as soon as you move in. It's part of the rituals around here, his own way of getting to know each tenant. The only one he never invited was Paolo. . . ."

"Perhaps I'll show him some of my poems."

Stanley Gendzel arched one of his extravagant eyebrows. "He'd be utterly delighted, **I'm sure**. That's the right attitude to take with that old lecher! He's working on some Japanese translations right now, y'know. Had some Japanese nobility up there helping him out. Flew her all the way from Toyko. Called her Camembert for short. She called him Daddybear."

The only thing I had when I moved in was a sorry-ass little suitcase crammed with notebooks and journals, a pair of jeans or two, and a memory of my mother Consuelo's face when I went out the door of her house. When I finally telephoned to say I was all right, Auntie Greta picked up the phone and answered in a solemn voice, "Good evening . . .the Sand Residence."

"Hello? Auntie Greta?" My own voice seemed unusually high to me.

"My dear George—are you all right?"

"Yes. I got a place—my own apartment. Is Mom there?"

"Your mother can't come to the phone, dear. She's not feeling well," Auntie Greta said.

"You mean she won't talk to me."

He cleared his throat. "Let's just say your mother is under sedation—high blood pressure, you know. She couldn't handle your leaving us too well."

"Well, tell her I'm all right. I'm living on Webster Street," I said.

"Webster Street??? Webster Street and what???"

"Oh, you know—near the freeway," I replied. I knew what was coming.

"Dios mio! You're living in **that** part of town?" Even Auntie Greta couldn't bring himself to say it: the ghetto. Bodies bleeding on the front steps of my building, virile young things with guns as erect as their dicks, leaping in and out of Chinese grocery stores. My mother's darkest fears.

I sighed. "Don't worry, Auntie Greta. There's a famous person living in this building. His name is Silver Daddy. He's my landlord."

"I've never heard of him," Auntie Greta said.

"Of course not," I retorted, exasperated. "You don't read the papers, except for the movie listings. Mom doesn't read the papers, either. Well, if you did, you might know about his column in the Sunday arts section. He writes on all the new stuff going on in the art world."

Auntie Greta was obviously offended. "Well, I don't know about that, young lady. I do read the paper from time to time! I know you've always thought yourself above us."

"Oh jesus, there you go sounding like my mother," I said.

"You know what they say—association makes for assimilation. Listen, George, do you have enough locks on your doors and windows?"

"Yes."

"I'll break the news to your mother gently. And please, dear, keep in touch. Are you getting a phone?"

"No. But there's a pay phone in the lobby," I said.

"A **pay** phone! In the **lobby**! OH MY GOD!" Auntie Greta groaned.

I figured it was better if I hung up first.

Family matters resolved for the moment, I called Boogie's brother's house next. His brother tersely informed me that Boogie had moved out recently and was now living a wild and sinful life under the care of some cocaine freak from Tokyo named Prince Genji.

"You could say he's doing real well," Boogie's brother said sarcastically. I knew he had never liked me anyway, so I stopped worrying about it. "I'm sure he'd love to hear from you. Maybe you can help him out on his project."

"Project? Boogie's working?" I was amazed.

"You could call it that. Here—" his brother said, giving me Boogie's new phone number. "Give him a ring. And don't forget to say hello to him for me."

I cheered up. "Why sure. I'll be glad to—"

"George," he interrupted, "you can also tell that faggot brother of mine that I'm through. His whole family washes their hands of him. You understand? We never want to see him again."

This time, Boogie's brother hung up on me first.

Welcome to de Ghetto

From my new apartment window, I watched Silver Daddy stroll down the street. He wore a leather cowboy vest that accentuated the paunchy belly that jutted out as he walked. There was something grand about the way he swaggered, in spite or because of his weight. Like a futuristic Santa Claus so sure of himself he sees nothing, he stopped under my window and called up to me, his icy blue eyes twinkling and his silver moustache gleaming. Ho-ho-ho.

"Are you the new tenant?"

"Yes. My name is George Sand."

"I know," Silver Daddy said. "Stanley told me. This is all very interesting. You must come to dinner this evening and meet my family."

I seemed to have no choice in the matter. We arranged a suitable time, and he strolled away, turning around halfway up the block to tell me that my new neighborhood would be a good education for me.

"Bleeding bodies happen almost everyday in America," Silver Daddy said ominously. "You simply must face up to it, George."

Persimmons

Tinkerbelle, Silver Daddy's secretary–companion, led me into the dining room of Silver Daddy's spacious ghetto penthouse. A wooden refectory table was set for four people with earth-toned Japanese bowls and ivory chopsticks. A slender vase filled with white chrysanthemums stood at the center of the table. Chinese masks and cubist paintings by Silver Daddy hung on the walls. Navajo baskets and Nigerian carvings were strewn haphazardly but deliberately around the room.

Tinkerbelle watched me with curious detachment as I wandered around, politely studying Silver Daddy's rather bland attempts at painting. Tinkerbelle was in her early thirties, a small-boned woman with shoulder-length brown hair and horn-rimmed glasses. She was wearing her standard uniform: nondescript plaid skirt, white Ladybug shirt, and a conservative cardigan sweater. Everything about her was mousey, but she emitted a certain nervous energy as she scurried around the room, chain-smoking Gauloise cigarettes. Bored with the paintings and artifacts, I decided to be friendly and start a conversation.

"Are you the one helping Silver Daddy out with the translations?" I asked her.

Tinkerbelle seemed rather offended. "Have you been talking to the tenants? If so, you've been grossly misinformed. I am Silver Daddy's secretary—his right hand, so to speak. I sometimes also do the cooking for him," she added, primly.

"Oh," I said, immediately intimidated by her Dame Edith Evans manner.

"Silver Daddy is a gourmet chef, among other things," Tinkerbelle continued, with a great deal of pride. "He taught me how to cook international dishes. I hope you like sushi."

"It's actually one of my favorites," I said.

"Good. We're having a complete Japanese menu tonight: miso soup, sushi, sashimi, and daikon. Silver Daddy's on one of his kicks."

Suddenly, Silver Daddy's precocious, fourteen-year-old daughter grand-jeteed into the room. An aspiring ballerina with feline green eyes and long dark hair pulled back into a ponytail, she wore a pink tutu, pink tights, and pink satin toeshoes. She held out her hand and spoke with a puzzling accent that constantly shifted from French to Bela Lugosi pseudo-Hungarian.

27

"Good evening," she said, "you must be George. My name is Porno. I'm Silver Daddy's teenage daughter."

I shook her hand. "Pleased to meet you," I said, somewhat startled.

"**AND HERE HE IS, LADIES . . . AMERICA'S OLDEST LIVING LEGEND: MY ESTEEMED FATHER, SILVER DADDY!!!**" Porno announced brightly, like an emcee in some decadent Berlin cabaret.

Tinkerbelle bowed as if on cue, and I followed suit. Silver Daddy sauntered into the room, wearing a long black kimono, with a red sash tied around his Sumo wrestler waist.

I handed him a gift-wrapped package, trimmed with origami birds. "I brought you some persimmons."

He sized me up slowly with his icy blue eyes. "DELIGHTFUL! Remind me to tell you one of my persimmon anecdotes someday. You know what they taste like, don't you?"

"No," I said, shaking my head.

"**Japanese pussy,** of course!" He chuckled at his own joke. Porno and Tinkerbelle clapped their hands and laughed along with him. "Shall we sit down and have dinner?" Silver Daddy gestured towards the table. "You must tell us all about yourself, George."

We all sat down except Tinkerbelle. She flitted about like a dragonfly, serving the food, bringing dishes in and out of the room, smoking her endless cigarettes.

"You're named after **the** George Sand, aren't you?" Silver Daddy asked me.

"Actually, my parents thought they were being funny. I don't think they had any idea who she really was," I replied.

Silver Daddy frowned. "How **painful.** Have you ever read any of her novels?"

"No."

"Oh, you **must!**" Porno chimed in. "I read all her work by the time I was twelve."

Unimpressed by his daughter's enthusiasm, Silver Daddy pointedly ignored her. "At least read her biography," he advised me. "There are some good ones available these days. You may find it illuminating. She was a most interesting personality—particularly when she ran around with that musician Chopin!" He paused. "I hope you brought your work."

I hesitated before answering. "I did. I wasn't sure if I should, but—"

"Don't be silly," Silver Daddy interrupted. "**I expected you to.** How do you like the miso soup? Tinkerbelle made it herself, from scratch."

"It's organic," Porno said, with the same enthusiasm. "Soybean's the best thing for you. I was raised on it. Wasn't I, Daddy?"

"Yes," Silver Daddy sighed. He turned to me. "Her mother was a health food fanatic. Died at an early age."

"**No, she didn't!**" Porno declared, visibly annoyed. "You're always saying that! Mama is alive and well in Arizona. Your **first** wife died at an early age. In childbirth, I believe," Porno added, with a hint of irony.

"Having a baby is like shitting a giant watermelon," Tinkerbelle suddenly intoned, sitting down at the table. She nibbled at her sushi.

"I wouldn't know," I murmured, blushing.

"Well, that's all right," Porno said, " 'cause Tinkerbelle knows. Tinkerbelle likes to think she's an authority on all subjects—don't you, Tinker, dear?"

"It's your father's influence," Tinkerbelle replied coolly. "Have some more sashimi, Porno."

In a mournful, basso profundo voice, Silver Daddy began chanting:

There was a young man
from St. John's
who went out to bugger
the swans,
when up stepped the porter
who said, "Take my daughter—
them swans is reserved
for the dons."

Once more, Tinkerbelle and Porno applauded and giggled. "Daddy, you're getting more academic in your old age," Porno said.

"It's difficult having a movie star for a daughter," Silver Daddy said, stiffly.

I looked at the smiling Porno. "I didn't know you were in the movies."

"We don't talk about it much around here," Porno said. "Daddy forbids it."

"I only forbid it because I'm not sure of my feelings," Silver Daddy said. "You're only fourteen years old. What would your mother have said if she knew? She's probably turned over in her grave by now."

Porno began pouting, her full, luscious lower lip trembling with emotion. "There you go again," she accused her father. "Mama's not dead. Your first wife is dead. Mama lives in Arizona. And she doesn't care about me, one way or the other."

Gazing at me with her green cat-eyes, she said, "Daddy likes to think he's ahead of his time, but he can't cope with the fact that I make pornographic movies."

"Is that how you got your name?" I asked, losing my appetite.

"Yes. It's my stage name. **I hate my real name.** Can you imagine someone as hip as Silver Daddy calling his daughter RUTH?"

"May I have some more sushi, please?" I asked Tinkerbelle, trying to conceal my embarrassment. All I'd wanted was a good meal and a positive start in my career.

"Have as much as you want," Silver Daddy said grandly. "I love young girls with hearty appetites."

"You certainly do," Porno said.

"RUTH!" Silver Daddy barked, his icy blue eyes crackling. "You're getting out of hand. I wish you'd **shut up**."

29

I started to get up from the table. "Maybe I should leave. . . ."

Tinkerbelle was horrified. "You can't do **that**. You haven't finished your dinner."

"Certainly not," Silver Daddy agreed. "**I won't allow it!** Don't let family intrigues spoil the evening for us, George." He took a deep breath. "NOW—it's time for my persimmons."

I sat back down. Tinkerbelle handed Silver Daddy the bowl of persimmons.

Silver Daddy attacked the persimmons, slurping noisily and lasciviously. Once in a while he would look at me meaningfully. Porno watched her father eat the fruit with a dreamy look in her eyes.

"Daddy, do you know the title of my next film?"

He never stopped eating. "WHAT?" he grunted.

"**Persimmons!** I thought of you right away." She paused, but when her father didn't react she began directing her comments to me. "I'm going to star in the loveliest film," she began, in her childlike, faraway voice. "I shall lie spread-eagled on top of a concert grand piano, and my mouth shall remain open throughout the entire movie. See my mouth? I've been told I have the most sensuous mouth since Ingrid Bergman in **Notorious**—don't I, Daddy?"

Silver Daddy reached for another persimmon.

"Two Arabian stallions prance around the room, their luxurious manes occasionally brushing against my extremely sensitive nipples," Porno said, a slight smile at the corners of her mouth. "The opening scene will be shot in slow motion, of course, with lots of diffused light and all that sort of thing. Then, Van Cliburn enters the room, totally unaware that I'm lying naked on his grand piano, and proceeds to play an extremely tacky rendition of 'Moonlight Sonata.'"

"Hmmm. One of my favorites," I murmured.

"Would you like some tea, or coffee?" Tinkerbelle asked me. "Coffee."

Tinkerbelle scurried out of the room, puffing on her Gauloise cigarette.

". . .As I writhe sinuously atop the concert grand," Porno went on, by now oblivious to everyone, "a leering Aubrey Beardsley-type dwarf waddles into the room, carrying a dome-covered silver platter. He removes the dome to reveal a quivering, asthmatic anteater. The anteater, of course, has no idea what's going on. He crinkles his snout in the direction of my gaping, nubile honeypot."

I was so mesmerized by this scenario that I was unaware of Tinkerbelle at my elbow, pouring coffee in my cup. Porno seemed like she was going deeper into a trancelike state.

"I lift up one leg in agonizing slow-motion, as the anteater's tongue slithers slowly out. The whole thing is going to be choreographed like an excruciating, torrid ballet—by me, of course. . . ."

"I didn't realize you were so talented," I said.

She ignored me. "The sticky tip of the anteater's tongue explore my

swollen clitoris, and I arch my supine back as the leering dwarf giggles. Van Cliburn sweats as the music crescendoes, his hair in electric shock reminiscent of Elsa Lanchester in **Bride of Frankenstein**. The anteater, disappointed at having found no ants, turns away from my juicy honeypot and is suddenly grabbed by the leering dwarf, who by this time has an enormous hard-on."

She paused, and for a moment her cat's eyes focused on me. "You know, little men have the biggest dicks, sometimes."

She said this with a combination of innocence and matter-of-factness that reminded me of my friend Boogie.

"The leering dwarf pulls down his knickers and buggers the struggling anteater, who can't escape the dwarf's powerful embrace," Porno said, panting excitedly. "Van Cliburn, oblivious to everything around him, is still crescendoing as five West Indians calypso into the room."

I gulped my coffee.

"Ahhh," Silver Daddy said, sucking on another persimmon, "**neo-colonialism**! The fucker and fuckee."

Neo-Colonialism

"The first West Indian has a dick that's long and thin, like a buffalo's," Porno said, breathlessly. "He enters me in the usual missionary position. I moan. He comes fast, like a junkie. The second West Indian has a dick that's pointy, like a Masai spear. He turns me over—quickly, quickly—and enters me from behind, humping me like a horse. No, no," she gasped, "not like a horse! Like an angry wolf!"

"An angry wolf **in heat**," Silver Daddy added, solemnly.

Porno nodded in agreement, her green eyes glittering. "He pulls out and comes all over Van Cliburn's elegant, brand-new tuxedo. Van Cliburn doesn't care, he continues his 'Moonlight Sonata' crescendo. The third West Indian has a dick that's not too long, but rather thick and awesome. I can't wait. He wraps my legs around his broad shoulders and proceeds to fuck me DEEP, with long, masterful strokes. By this time, the leering Beardsleyesque dwarf has rolled underneath the grand piano, grunting like a sow as he buggers the terrified anteater. Meanwhile, the fourth West Indian places his hook-shaped dick into my luscious, foaming, strawberry mouth."

"More coffee?" Tinkerbelle poured me a second cup.

"Thank you," I said. "It's very good."

"It's Blue Mountain coffee," Tinkerbelle informed me. "Silver Daddy

orders it especially from Jamaica."

Porno had shut her eyes, looking more ethereal than ever. "The fifth West Indian is a beautiful, degenerate fawn—the only other **star** in the film. He sucks my prominent, aching nipples as he beats off his dick, which happens to be the longest, thickest, most cobralike dick anybody would ever want to see. By this time, I am shrieking and gasping for breath—in between dicks and tongues in my mouth, my honeypot, and god-knows-where-else!"

She opened her eyes. "The fifth West Indian finally comes—like Niagara Falls—a never-ending stream on my breasts, my eyes, and my warm creamy belly. He wipes his dick in my long straight hair, murmuring endearments in Spanish, Portuguese, French, and patois. Van Cliburn finally collapses, like a ragdoll on his piano stool. The leering dwarf reaches a violent orgasm, trangling the puzzled and terrified anteater."

Silver Daddy smiled at no one in particular. "Salvador Dali enters the room, unlocking a cage filled with yellow butterflies—"

"Yes!" Porno exclaimed, radiant. "The butterflies hover over my sleeping body in the still, now-empty room. The film ends."

No one said anything much after that. Tinkerbelle had settled into a smoke-filled reverie of her own, and Silver Daddy retreated into his bed-room with my manuscripts. After my fourth cup of coffee, I excused myself and went downstairs to my apartment. They didn't bother to say goodnight.

My apartment was really a one-room studio, with a dingy closet of a kitchen and a gloomy bathroom where the roaches liked to hide. The best thing about it was the bathtub, a massive boat with lion's paws that had definitely seen better days. I loved filling it with warm water and just sitting in it for hours, thinking. Unhappy with the mattress on the floor I was using to sleep on, I had even considered turning my wonderful bath-tub into a bed.

I had left the apartment pretty much in the same state I had found it—the floor littered with papers of every shape and size, including news-papers. Almost all the papers belonged to the poet Paolo, although lately I had gotten in the habit of discarding my poems and stories in the same way—using the sheets of paper as rugs, haphazard decorations on the floor that floated in the air when the wind blew through the apartment.

I had taken to tacking some of my poems, finished and unfinished, on the walls next to or on top of the poems Paolo had glued on like wallpaper. In an eerie way, it made me feel safe and comfortable.

I called Boogie and invited him to see my new home. He seemed highly amused by my surroundings as soon as he walked through the door. I was impressed by his appearance—Boogie had always been very pretty, and his multicultural looks confused a lot of people. He could pass for Latino, Asian, even Native American. His eclectic way of dressing never betrayed the toughness behind the elegance, and I loved the way his beauty drove men and women crazy. Nothing seemed to disturb him, an attribute that could sometimes make me angry. But when I was feeling good about myself, I could think of no one else in the world whose opinion mattered more.

Boogie in the Palace

Boogie came from a hardworking, lower-middleclass family that always found it difficult to make ends meet. I suppose that's why he was so clever at putting old clothes together into what he called his "costumes." I stared curiously at the expensive silk scarf around his neck and the custom-made snakeskin boots he wore on his feet. He sat down on a stack of books. "Really, George. It amazes me how you can live here," he said with a smile.

"It's my own place, Boogie. I've never had one."

"Hey, remember the first time I met you? In that fucked-up high school we went to?"

"Yeah. How can I forget, you asshole?" I said, lounging on the mattress next to where he sat. "You called me a cunt."

We both laughed. "Hey, I thought you wuz such a fox," Boogie said. "**Really**. You're one of the few women I've ever considered fucking."

"Oh, **please**," I groaned, "the way you talk, you'd think you were a million years old. You don't even know that many women!"

"Okay then, maybe you're the only woman I've ever considered fucking—and I'm eternally grateful for the passing desire."

"I'll bet."

"Anyway, I saw you sashaying down the hall carrying your books and lookin' so outta place. . . . 'Shit,' I said to myself, 'that looks like another pinoy!' I was so sick of bein' the only Filipino in that goddam school . . . y'know what I mean? I wasn't even fashionable!"

"You haven't changed. Is that all you care about?"

"Seriously, George," Boogie said, "bloods were **in** that year. Remember? Civil rights, Martin Luther King, and all the white girls fucking the black dudes? Remember Pamela Wolfe's birthday party?"

"I wasn't invited," I said, "but I went with you. You were so popular."

He was obviously pleased. "Of course I was! Life of the party, best dancer in school—"

"The most promising musician," I said, remembering our high school yearbook.

"Pamela Wolfe referred to us as 'spades'—I guess cuz we hung around the bloods all the time. 'Oh, Boogie,'" Boogie mimicked Pamela Wolfe's whiney voice, "'you've gotta come to my party!' She was always pushing her big tits in my face . . . 'Bring all your James Brown records and all the spades you know!' God! The nerve of that woman," he said, enjoying himself.

"It wasn't so long ago," I said. "You talk like it was ages and ages ago."

"Well, it is to me," Boogie retorted sharply. He got up and started pacing around the room, wired. "If I never see those people again, I'll be just fine," he muttered. "Especially Pamela Wolfe."

"She was a real liberal," I said, in an attempt to lighten up his sudden change of mood. His expensive clothes and temperamental nature were all new to me.

"Yeah, but it was all a game to her. Let's not talk about her anymore. It's boring," he said.

His brusqueness hurt my feelings. "No one knew you were a faggot then," I said, sarcastically. "They just thought you danced well."

Boogie stopped pacing and looked at me, smiling again. "You cunt."

"THAT, I believe, was the first word you ever said to me. You walked up to me in the hallway and stared me up and down. Then you flashed that famous smile, showing me your pearly white teeth. 'PUKI,' you said to me in Tagalog."

"That's right, sweetheart. I wanted to get a **reaction**."

"So where'd you get all the fancy clothes?" I suddenly asked, taking him by surprise.

A full-length mirror hung on my closet door. Boogie stared at his reflection. "I never thought you'd ask," he said. "This involves you—so pay attention. One day, as I was prowling the streets looking for some action, a car pulled up. It was a little sportscar driven by a young woman who looked just like Billie Holiday. She even wore a gardenia in her hair. She introduced herself as Cinderella."

"Cinderella?"

"Uh-huh. She was very pleasant, George—and softspoken. She seemed to know all about me. And **you**."

"Weren't you paranoid? Maybe she's a cop."

Boogie looked annoyed. "Oh honey, STOP. I know a cop when I see one—better than you ever could. I've been dealing with them all my life," he said with pride. "You don't know nothin' about that, where you come from."

It was my turn to get annoyed. "And what the fuck is that supposed to mean?"

Boogie put his hands on my shoulders, massaging them gently. "There you go again. Relax," he said, soothing me with his voice. "Is it true, or isn't it true that maybe your daddy plays golf with the president back in the islands every once in a while?"

"He can't stand the president, too, you know—" I said, angry with myself for feeling guilty.

"I'm sure he can't," Boogie said, drily, "but for all the wrong reasons. The president probably can't tell the difference between a salad fork and a soup spoon. Remember that story you once told me? Your father got invited to some official function at the palace and he refused to go—what was it he said?"

I started giggling. "He said—'My dear, I've been invited by a better class of people, in my time.'"

"Exactly!" Boogie declared, a look of triumph on his face.

"I was disappointed," I said. "I thought it would make a good story. Father goes to banquet with corrupt politicians. Gossips with Lady Macbeth, compliments her on her jewels."

"Of course you were, George. And don't give me that shit about your writing! You wanted your father to go to the palace for the same reason we all want to go to the palace! To rub elbows with some real **power**—"

"That's not true." I shook my head slowly. Boogie stopped massaging my shoulders and sat next to me on the mattress.

"You're lying again, George. Don't think I don't know. Your mother would admit it. She doesn't mind being crass," he said.

"But I do," I said, in a small voice.

He put his arm around me. "That's all I'm trying to tell you, sweetheart. Even your mother knows more about this shit than you do. She came from a poor family and married into money, right? That's why she hates me. I remind her of her family."

"How do you know? You were born in America. You've never even been home," I said.

"All I have to do is listen to my father talk in his broken English," Boogie said, wearily. "Look at his worn-out hands. See my mother's shy and frightened face whenever she gets on a bus. They're permanent immigrants in this lousy place, and I've stopped asking myself why they even bothered. I imagine the Philippines. I have a fertile imagination, George. You always used to say that."

I said nothing. Boogie tightened his grip on my shoulder for a second, then let me go. "I've hurt your feelings. I'm sorry—and all I wanted to do was tell you how I got these clothes," he said with a sad smile.

Guerrillas

I ignored Boogie's attempts to soothe me. "When I go home, back to the islands to visit my father, the same movie unfolds in my head."

Boogie prodded me gently. "What movie?"

36

"The one where they're gonna come and kill everyone in the house," I replied. "And I'll just happen to be there, by chance—except deep in my heart I know that it's all part of my destiny." I paused, looking at Boogie's chiselled, inscrutable face.

"There are three bedrooms in my father's house," I said, "and my grandmother, who is paralyzed, sleeps in the first bedroom at the top of the stairs. My grandmother is totally helpless, so a nurse has been hired to remain at her side twenty-four hours a day. My grandmother is fed intravenously and shits into a sack that's attached to her side. She clutches a rosary in her gnarled, arthritic hands—mumbling incoherent prayers to herself. No one understands her, but everyone goes on about what a true saint she is. Her eyes are glazed, and she doesn't seem to recognize any of us."

"My god,—" Boogie took my hand. I held on to it tightly.

"It's true," I said. "I'm not lying this time, Boogie. I like to imagine that my grandmother's already left her skeletal little body, that she exists on a high spiritual plane. In my movie, they kill the nurse first, but they never touch my grandmother. In fact, they seem to be afraid of my grandmother. After the massacre, she's the only survivor left—bobbing up and down in her wheelchair, mumbling and clutching the rosary beads in her hands."

"Who are **they**, George?" Boogie asked, although he knew.

"The revolutionaries. The guerrillas—yes, I prefer calling them guerrillas," I said. "It's so much more accurate." We sat in silence for a while, and I didn't let go of his hand. "I sleep in the second bedroom. I hear them in the next room, killing the nurse quietly and efficiently. I lay in my bed, sweating and staring at the door. Should I try to escape? I ask myself over and over again. I can hear the leaves rustling. The night is alive with insects chirping and lizards hissing outside my window. It's unbearably hot, even in the middle of the night. I am unable to move, sweating and trembling underneath my thin blanket. I hear soft movements in the next room, one low and muffled cry. I go over the movie again and again in my head. The night the guerrillas come to my father's house. I even imagine the face of the killer."

"Stop it, George. I can't listen to this anymore," Boogie said, letting go of my hand and getting up from the bed. He walked over to the mirror and stared at his reflection once more. His face was like stone, and he could see me reflected, on the mattress directly behind him.

"But you must," I said, "because it's all true. A vision of the future."

Boogie walked over to the window and stared out at the street. "No. You're wrong. It's one vision of the future, and it's your own particular paranoia that's taken you there."

"The killer is a beautiful young man," I said. "He looks like you, Boogie. High cheekbones, smooth copper-colored skin, straight blue black hair. His lovely eyes pierce the darkness in my bed as he finds me, cowering. He bends his sullen face towards mine. I am gazing into his glistening black eyes, thinking of my father sleeping in the third bedroom. I am sure the young man is going to kiss me, but he slits my throat instead. Quietly and efficiently. I've been spared hearing my father die—"

Boogie was visibly shaken. "Jesus christ! I think you've taken too much acid. Relax! Don't be so hard on yourself! Listen, everyone has a choice," Boogie said, trying to convince himself. "To see what they wanna see. To be what they wanna be. It's all very simple. I mean, I know what you're talkin' about—but I don't wanna be reminded of it **all the time!**"

I avoided his eyes. "I'm sorry."

He grinned. "It's okay, it's okay—we're both tripping heavy, that's all."

"Hey, you want some coffee?" I asked, smiling back at him. "It's all I have."

"No, thanks. Maybe I should run out and get us a bottle of wine. Calm you down," Boogie said.

I started crying very quietly. He took me in his arms. "Oh god," I said, my face pressed into the collar of his fancy new shirt, "I feel so silly."

"You shouldn't feel silly. And I'm sorry for saying those things about your parents. It was cruel and stupid," Boogie said.

"Sometimes I think I'm in love with you," I confessed, tears streaming down my face.

Boogie kissed my wet cheek. "I think I'm in love with you too—sometimes. Feel better? Want me to get you some water?" He seemed nervous about what he'd just said and rushed out of the room, busying himself in my pathetic little kitchen. He came back with a glass of cloudy water.

"Tell me where you got your clothes," I said.

"Well, it's all very convoluted, but I've got this patron right now, who I met through Cinderella. He has me working on a project," Boogie said.

"What kind of project?"

"It's really **our** project, George—that's why I was so glad when you finally called me up tonight! I'd been thinking about you, but I didn't want to call your house and get your mother on the phone. I want you to get involved in it. It could be the biggest break in our lives," Boogie said, gravely. He pulled a small vial out of his shirt pocket. "Here. I got something for us."

"Cocaine? How'd you manage to pay for this?" I leaned over as he put the silver spoon up my nose.

"My benefactor. You must meet him—he's a very generous man. Our favorite drug—," Boogie chortled with glee. "This should bring you up. Really, George. I don't like seeing you morose like this. It's creepy."

"I'm not being morose," I retorted, snorting more coke. "I'm just being dramatic."

"Well, save the drama for our project," Boogie said, excitement mounting in his voice. I didn't know if it was the coke or this new project, but I hadn't seen Boogie excited like this in a long time. Except maybe the first time we both hitchhiked to Monterey for the Pop Festival, and experienced Jimi Hendrix.

38

Guitars / Shooting Stars

The first time we saw Jimi Hendrix perform, we thought we were hallucinating—watching him slash his burning guitar onstage, making love to it as if it were a woman.

It might have been his face or hair, I'm not sure. Or the way he looked slightly uncomfortable on stage, holding his guitar awkwardly, yet playing it with the clarity and authority of one who knows his instrument completely, inside and out.

We were in our last year of high school—1967. I had gotten very close to Leopoldo Makaliwanag, who called himself "Boogie." He invited me to hitchhike to Monterey for the Pop Festival with him, with maybe fifteen dollars between us. No tickets to any of the concerts, but a lot of faith.

I wanted to be there for the sun and the crazy, technicolor atmosphere. Boogie was there for the music. He was ready to offer his services to the festival promoters, in exchange for free tickets to the concerts. Clean-up guy, security guard, gopher, anything. . . .

At night we huddled in a sleeping bag next to the Hell's Angels campsite. No one took us seriously, not even the bikers. We were two wayward Filipino kids in torn jeans and tattered velvet shirts. Our second-hand coats offered no protection against the fierce Monterey nights, but what did we care? It was a chance to see and hear Otis Redding—plus a new band from England led by some guitar player named Jimi Hendrix.

They were scheduled for the last night of the festival. When Jimi came out onstage, we couldn't believe our eyes. People stood on their folding chairs to get a better look. Who was this outrageous black man with the crazy hair and those two foreign-looking white boys in the background as his **sidemen**???

He wasn't Otis Redding. Everyone felt safe about loving him.

He wasn't even Little Richard. Everyone could dismiss him as some legendary rock n' roll faggot.

He was Jimi Hendrix—sticking his pretty pink tongue out at all the women in the audience, maybe even the men. 1967. Flower-power time. Not the time for ambiguous sexual dilemmas.

Boogie and I stood up on our chairs to get a better look, like everyone else. Jimi's hair stood out from his head like a crown of flames. He seemed painfully shy, his brash talk onstage seemed like a cover-up for his apparent terror when he wasn't playing the guitar.

Boogie was mesmerized by this black apparition piercing the cold night air with the silver arrows of his guitar. "He's afraid they won't accept him," Boogie whispered in my ear. "That's why he's overdoing it." Then Boogie sighed. "Ooh, I can't stand it," he murmured. "This music is terrifying."

"Isn't he lovely?"

We both agreed.

Boogie and I were both getting speedy, taking countless turns snorting up the blow. I could tell he was enjoying having excellent drugs at his disposal and enough cash in his pocket to take taxis everywhere and buy me bottles of wine and cognac.

"You'll never believe it, George—it's too grand," Boogie laughed. "Like I was saying earlier, I met this mysterious woman Cinderella. Turns out she knows all about us—how talented we both are. I figured she was some big freak who hung out in the music scene and liked young boys. But she's not—not at all! She's a free-lance agent of some sort. For this prince."

"What kinda prince?"

"A Japanese prince named Genji. Lives in this palatial flat downtown. He's young, and oh-so pretty," Boogie sighed, a sly smile on his face. "Buys me all my clothes. Pays the rent. Loves to get high."

"Sounds too good to be true."

"Nothing wrong with it, George. It's legit. I work for him, in a sense. He wants to finance a musical, see. And I've been commissioned to write the music. You're the perfect person to write the lyrics and the story. Genji's got the concept. We're gonna blow everybody's minds—y'know what I mean?"

How could I resist? I told him I'd be over to meet the prince the next afternoon.

Gardenias

Cinderella picked me up in her innocuous little green sportscar. She had been sent to take me to Prince Genji's house. "Get in," she ordered, her face obscured by the rhinestone-studded veil of a velvet pillbox hat. She was distant but polite, smiling at me occasionally as she drove expertly down the freeway.

"Prince Genji is eager to meet you," she said, smoothly. "I'm sure you'll get along with him quite well."

"I can't wait."

"The most important thing is to remember how committed the prince is to this project, and how much he expects out of you and Boogie."

"I really don't know much about it," I said.

"The prince will be happy to tell you everything," Cinderella said. "I only work for the prince."

Somehow when she said that I didn't quite believe her, but I decided not to say anything. We drove along in silence the rest of the way, and I studied Cinderella stealthily. Something about her—the way she sat up straight, for example, holding her head regally like a swan—made me quiet and somehow put me in my place. She reminded me of some imperious facets of my mother. Two gardenias were pinned to the bosom of her silver dress.

Prince Genji

The butler led me into Prince Genji's opulent living room. Jimi Hendrix's "Are You Experienced?" was blasting through the giant speakers. A grand piano stood in one corner, next to huge bay windows that looked out into a garden. The floor was covered with plush, thousand-year-old Persian and Chinese rugs. Emerald-green plants hung from the ceiling, and cobra orchids filled the black vases scattered around the room. A collection of gold and silver fans was displayed on one wall, and the marbletop coffee-table was littered with cocaine and assorted paraphernalia: razorblades, straws, packs of matches, and tiny spoons.

Prince Genji was lounging on the sofa, lazily watching Boogie dance to the jagged metallic music through half-opened eyelids. Occasionally he nodded his head in time to the music, but Genji was obviously in a stoned stupor—
a half-smile on his serene, girlish face.

They were oblivious to our presence, and for the longest time the butler and I stood in the doorway.

Boogie flaunted his hips in front of the sleepy-eyed prince. "OOH—will you listen to that, Genji! Have you ever heard anything so low?"

"Certainly not."

"A vision for the future, Genji! A vision for the universe!"

Prince Genji looked bored. "I'm nodding out."

"You mustn't nod out, Genji—it's too early! For godsake, I'm all hyped up! I'm about to give birth to an idea. Shit, that's what's wrong with you people!"

Prince Genji shot Boogie a warning glance. "Are you going to bring up the war again?" he asked, defensively.

"I was talkin' about aristocrats, fool," Boogie retorted, dancing over to the record player. He played the same song by Hendrix over and over, as if he couldn't get enough of it. "You constantly bring up these projects, Genji—wonderful projects, I might add—but when you get right down to it, you're just blithering away, at my expense," Boogie added, cockily.

"**At your expense?** Who's paying the rent around here? Who's giving you a place to stay? Who clothes you and feeds you? Who believes in your musical talents?" Prince Genji demanded.

Boogie stopped dancing and looked at the angry prince. "You do."

"And don't you forget it."

The tense silence was broken by Boogie, who sat next to the prince and smiled seductively at him. "Well, as I was saying, Genji, we've got to get started on this musical. My head is just swimming with ideas."

The prince yawned. "Why don't you snort some heroin and cool down? There's plenty of time for all that." Genji bent over and touched Boogie's face, ready to kiss him.

The butler cleared his throat, his eyes fixed on the floor.

Genji looked up, annoyed. "Yes, Esteban. **What is it?**"

"You have a guest, Prince Genji," the tuxedo-clad eunuch announced. "Cinderella dropped her off. She claims to be a friend of Senorito Boogie's, whom she keeps referring to as **Leopoldo**."

"That's my Christian name, dear," Boogie said, coldly.

Prince Genji was amused. "Calm down, Boogie. GOODNESS! I'm sure Esteban didn't mean to offend you. Did you, Esteban?" The butler was silent. "Well, Esteban, show the young lady in."

I was shy and nervous, intimidated by the luxuriousness of the surroundings. The beautiful young men stared at me, like two preening leopards purring before the kill.

"You are prettier than I expected," Genji cooed, suddenly kissing me on the neck. He pulled up my shirt and kissed my belly. "I love to kiss. Kissing is the most exquisite movement of the mouth. Have you had lunch?"

"I'm sure food is the last thing on her mind, Genji! Let's talk business," Boogie snapped.

Genji was tickled by Boogie's jealousy. "Certainly, Boogie. Come, dear George. We don't want to offend your friend. Pull your shirt down."

"Let's get high," Boogie said.

Genji pulled on a bellcord, and the butler entered the room. "Esteban, bring me my potions and vials." The butler bowed and exited. "George, come sit down next to me. Boogie tells me you're quite the poet."

"She is," Boogie gushed. "George, show him some of those lyrics we were working on."

I handed Genji my notebook, and the three of us sat in silence as Genji flipped through the notebook casually. "My, my . . . you have such a way with cliches, George," he finally said. "You make them palatable."

"I like working with the obvious," I said.

"And the not-so-obvious," Boogie added.

The butler brought in a silver tray, laden with bottles and little boxes and glassine envelopes. As quietly as he came, he swished out of the room.

"My potions!" Genji was delighted. "Finally. I can't work without them." He looked at me with a disconcerting warmth. "You wouldn't happen to know any riddles, would you? I love riddles. They keep my mind active."

Boogie was snorting away and getting bitchy. "Riddles? That's a new

42

one. I thought having houseguests gave your life meaning—"

"**Mind your manners, young man!** You don't know to whom you are speaking." Genji turned back to me. "I don't know how you put up with him. He's beautiful, but he really lacks breeding."

"I'm sure he didn't mean it."

"I'm sure he did," Genji retorted. "I may seem sheltered, but I'm not stupid."

Boogie got up and went to the piano. He sat down and stared at the keys for what seemed an eternity. Then he started playing.

"**Smokey Robinson?**" The prince spit out the name with contempt. "Is that all you know?"

"It's part of my Apollo Theater concept," Boogie said. "For the musical."

"Well, I wanted original tunes. That's what the public wants," Prince Genji said. He directed his next remark to me. "Boogie **thinks** he knows what the public wants. But what does he know about Broadway? He's never been out of California."

"Boogie didn't mention Broadway to me." I was surprised.

"That's typical. What did you think, my dear? That I was going to all this trouble just to finance some little-theater project?"

"Why us?" I asked. "We don't have any experience."

"Precisely. But you have the potential," Genji replied. "And that's what I'm banking on. Fresh meat. Young blood."

"Actually," Boogie said to me from across the room, "it's because he doesn't know anyone else."

I could barely suppress a giggle. Genji ignored us. "I want a combination of Kabuki, the Folies Bergere, Busby Berkeley, James Brown at the Apollo, and pornography. I want masks in red and black, and chorus lines of young virgins with blonde marcelled hair singing 'You Can't Take That Away from Me.' I want levels of meaning, most of all," Genji emphasized, his black eyes shining, "esoteric, obvious, spiritual, and vulgar—all at once! I have the means to produce this extravagant dream, but I don't have any connections."

"This is kinda wild," I said, hesitantly. "I mean, I've never been asked to do anything like this."

"Of course not, George!" Boogie said, growing impatient with me. "This is a major break. Don't listen to her, Genji. She's shy, but she can do it."

It was my turn to get angry. "STOP APOLOGIZING FOR ME. I'm trying to understand why."

Prince Genji looked puzzled. "**Why, what?**"

"Why you're doing all this," I said. "I mean, with your kinda money, you could invest in a sure thing. Musicals are so—"

"Chancey." Boogie finished my sentence for me.

"Yes," I agreed, "chancey. I mean, how do we know it's gonna work? What if you lose all your money in such a risky venture?"

"Risky venture, **indeed**!" Genji sniffed, giving me a haughty look.

"Would you rather I invested in oil, perhaps? Or coffeebeans? No one knows it, but the price of coffee is going UP. And we're going to have an oil crisis very soon. And how about commodities. Pork bellies and winter wheat. Grain futures. **Invisible things.** Don't you think I've done all that already? Pet food, for instance. Did you know that's a safe and sound investment? I'm surprised at you, George Sand."

"Why?"

"Because you're being so mundane this evening." Prince Genji and Boogie started laughing. I stared at them in disbelief, then got up from the couch.

"I'm leaving," I said. "I don't have to listen to this shit."

"Come on, George!" Boogie needled. "Can't you take a joke? You used to have such a sick sense of humor."

"Humor? You call his insults humor?" I looked at the smiling prince. "Thanks for an unpleasant evening."

"George, don't leave," Boogie pleaded, a frantic look in his eyes. "PLEASE."

"I don't know why I let you get away with so much shit," I said to him, wearily. Resigned, I sat back down. The prince offered me some more coke.

"George, I must apologize for my bad temper," Genji said. "It's the drugs, I'm sure. I get carried away sometimes. Don't I, Boogie?"

"Yeah. I was meaning to speak to you about it."

"You're quite a liar," Genji said, still smiling. "But we'll discuss that some other time. Now, George, will you participate in this glorious project and stop worrying about the risks I'm taking? That's none of your concern, really. You should write, let your imagination run free, and enjoy yourself. We're going to make artistic history."

"Think of the fun we'll have," Boogie said, "collaborating on a musical about people like us."

"It's never been done before, you must admit," Genji said.

I felt pressured and slightly abused. "All right. But I'm still a little confused about it," I sighed.

"How do you think I feel, being the bastard son of an emperor who is no longer fashionable?" Prince Genji gazed into my eyes. "My mother was a hostess at the Queen Bee Cabaret in Tokyo. My supposedly invincible father surrendered his country. My mother was paid off. I was sent to Europe to learn the western ways of life—Paris, Florence, London, and even Budapest!" He laughed. "Do you know who I am? I guess Boogie never told you, but I know you, George Sand. I know what's going through that head of yours—your little nightmares about Daddy. Don't you know I understand it all too clearly? We are quite alike, you and I."

"No, we're not."

"You'll find out, soon enough," Genji said. "Both of you remember this—there are reasons why we all came together. I could be skiing somewhere in Switzerland, you know."

44

"Why don't you, then?" I asked him. "Skiing's easier than dealing with us."

"DO NOT ABUSE ME," Genji said, coldly. "You may have talent, according to your friend here, but you don't know anything. You don't understand me, because you refuse to face your nightmares. And that's what this musical is all about. Our American nightmares." He chuckled. He left the room, leaving a chill behind him.

I was frightened and anxious to leave.

"Boogie—" I touched his arm.

Boogie was still staring off into the distance. The butler came into the room, dimming the lights and cleaning up the coffee table. Boogie patted my hand absent-mindedly. "Don't worry, babe. Everything's gonna be all right . . ."

Tender Vittles

"Rover, Rover . . . ," I called out softly. "This cat that is sometimes an animal and sometimes a man—where are you, Rover?"

Rover appeared suddenly, lounging like an alley cat on the fence next to my apartment building. I hadn't seen him since our first encounter, and I missed him terribly. He leaped down nimbly off the fence, landing directly in front of me and grinning.

"Oh, Rover, where've you been? I've got so much to tell you."

"Really? Hey, George, I got somethin' for you. Somethin' very important to me." He grabbed me and pulled me toward him, startling me at first. Then we started dancing around wildly on the sidewalk. I was puzzled by his behavior, but then I got caught up by the sheer exuberance of the moment.

"I know why I love you," Rover said, kissing me passionately.

"Why?"

"I'll never tell."

"I love you back," I said. "I need to see you more. So much has been happening since I last saw you. I'm working on this musical project."

"Tell me about it," Rover said, playfully.

We went upstairs to my apartment and made love for hours. I fell asleep. When I awoke the room was dark, and Rover had disappeared, leaving his white guitar behind him. A sheet of music paper lay on the pillow next to me:

Loving You Was Better Than Never At All
by Rover The Cat (BMI, ASCAP, MEOW)

A new song. I was overwhelmed by a sudden, terrible loneliness. I never had the chance to tell him about my musical project, and I was afraid I would never see him again. I got up from the disheveled bed, looked for my notebook, and began to write.

Cinderella

A roomful of snow-white angora kittens / mirrors / Little Richard's silver boots / Lady Murasaki combing Dorian Gray's hair / Aluminum-foil palm trees. / Lupé Velez holds a bullwhip in one delicate hand, cracking it over her head as a chorus line of male Cuban dancers, pre-Castro-Havana-Ricky Ricardo style, shimmy and shake—Hawaiian shirts tied in a knot at their gleaming, well-oiled chests.

I was writing in my studio when a coach pulled up in front of the building. I heard Stanley Gendzel three flights down, cursing and throwing a general fit. The elegant coach was driven by rodents wearing lace-cuffed velvet jackets and sequined knickers. Satin ribbons were tied to their tails.

"RATS!" Stanley shrieked. **"RATS DRIVING A COACH!** They'll copulate and multiply all over the building!" He began sobbing. "This is all I need."

The rats remained calm, ignoring Stanley's outbursts. They didn't seem to have the slightest interest in copulating all over tenement halls.

There was a knock at my door. A footman entered, wearing an oversized Halloween rat mask. "I have been sent by Cinderella to give you this," the footman said, handing me a vial of cocaine. "She wishes to thank you for the work you've done so far, on behalf of Prince Genji, her dearest client. She urges you to keep on writing."

"Thanks," I mumbled, staring at the large vial of coke in my hand.

"Always remember," the footman said, "the best is yet to come."

He exited with a flourish, gracefully and quietly. I was stunned. Pure coke. The best in the west. Better than any joint shared furtively in high school toilets. Better than any blot of acid from Stanford laboratories. Better than any heroin balloon. Better than so-called love. Better than dancing. Better than poetry. Almost as good as music, and almost better than real love. "Oh, Cinderella," I said to myself, "my guardian angel, Cinderella."

The Sphinx Winks

The coke made me fidgety and nervous—my heart beating wildly and my head brimming over with ideas, like an outer-space washing machine spinning round and round. I managed to walk over to my makeshift desk and type:

Dancers glide through the room, dressed like Carmen Miranda. Their glistening, parted red lips are frozen in eerie, perpetual smiles. They kick their legs high up in the air to silent music. The young men in loud Hawaiian shirts enter stage left. They are barefoot and shake rattles and maracas at the audience ominously, as if casting a spell.

A frenetic, soundless movie. The insides of my wired mind. In spite of my growing anxiety, I couldn't stop snorting more coke. Jimi Hendrix warbled, "And the gods / made love." I collapsed on the floor. My radio was on. The Temptations followed Hendrix:

> **Oooh / baby / I'm losing you . . . It's in the air /**
> **it's everywhere / oooh / baby / I'm losing you . . .**

The diabolic disc jockey, Ding Dong Daddy, hissed and cooed on the airwaves: "THAT WAS IT, BOYS AND GIRLS—A RUNAWAY HIT BY THE TEMPS! THE TIME IS EIGHT SECONDS TO ONE, AND THIS IS YOUR NUMBER ONE DJ, DING DONG DADDY, PLAYING THAT MUSIC TO YOUR HEART'S CONTENT, ON THE GRAVEYARD SHIFT OF YOUR MIND. HEH-HEH-HEH . . . A NUMBER ONE DJ WITH A RUNAWAY HIT . . . AND THE TIME, BOYS AND GIRLS, IS ONE O'CLOCK IN THE A.M. AND IT'S TOO LATE!" He laughed maniacally. "IT'S TOO LATE!"

I tried to sit up, but rolled over on the floor instead, drool forming on the edges of my mouth. A giant orange cat entered my room, sniffing around me as if looking for something important. The door to my studio opened quietly, and Cinderella tiptoed in, carrying a huge bowl of food for the huge orange cat. The cat growled and began tearing each fish-flavored kernel apart with his fangs.

Cinderella bent over me, slapping me awake. I could smell the faint odor of gardenias.

"Rover . . . ," I murmured. "Where's Rover?"

"You're going to be all right," she said, watching me carefully with her lavender painted eyes.

"My nose hurts."

"That's what you get for being so greedy."

"I got carried away," I groaned. I sat up, gingerly feeling my aching head, my arms, my back. "I was trying to finish this incredible scene with my exploding imagination, but I think I got ahead of myself."

Cinderella straightened up and headed for the door. "I must go now. You'll feel better in a little while. Wash out your nostrils with warm water and take some vitamins. I certainly hope you've learned your lesson. As for me, it's way past my bedtime, and I can't stay."

Her satin skirt rustled as she shut the door behind her. The big orange cat finished eating. He climbed out my window and perched on the ledge, watching me languidly, like some guardian of the tomb, through the night.

47

Letters from Home

My dearest daughter:

I am writing you from the rain forests of Mindanao, where I've decided to stay and continue my search for rare species of dragonflies, monarch butterflies, giant praying mantis, and tsetse flies. Everything here is black, black—even the butterflies. I never thought I'd see anything like this, except in Brazil or Africa.

How are you? I hope you are attending church regularly and keep in constant touch with your mother. She keeps sending me telegrams in the jungle, worrying about you.

If you ever decide to return to the islands, let me know and I'll send you a plane ticket. The guavas are exceptionally sweet this year.

Fondest regards,

Dad

June 4

Dearest Dad:

I am in the midst of writing a Broadway musical. Can you believe it? You always said a college education wasn't necessary.

I've been rather sick lately, but I think I'm okay now. Must've been something I ate. Oh, well.

I phone Mom from time to time, but lately I've been so busy, it's been difficult.

I don't feel like coming back to the islands. I also haven't been to church since I was thirteen, but of course you can't remember that far back.

Write soon.

Love,

George

June 6

Dearest George:

Why haven't you called me in over a month? I'm worried sick, and so is Auntie Greta. You can thank your lucky stars **and** Auntie Greta that I haven't called the police to check on you!

This is a ridiculous situation for a woman of my stature, and you're

48

really being **inconsiderate**. Move out of that ghetto. Get a telephone. For godsake, don't you think of anyone else but yourself and that friend of yours?

You know WHO I'm talking about!

Love,

Your Mother

P.S. Auntie Greta sends his best. He hasn't been doing too well lately.

(Enclosed with her letter were newspaper clippings: "**DRUG-CRAZED STUDENT JUMPS OUT WINDOW / THINKS HE IS GOD!**" "**JIMI HENDRIX DEAD!**" I left the clippings on my desk, and the headlines glared at me for several days. I finally threw them in the trash and felt better.)

The Gangster of Love

I went over to Prince Genji's flat to show him the first draft of the script. The butler ushered me into the living room and informed me that the prince was getting dressed to go out. "He'll be with you shortly. Please make yourself comfortable."

I noticed a tall, lean man in his thirties sitting in the shadows, puffing quietly on a hookah.

"How do you do, George? My name is Doctor T." His voice was soft and enticing, eyes concealed by dark sunglasses. He made me uncomfortable.

"I'm here to see the prince," I said curtly, ignoring his introduction.

"Mind your temper," he said, smiling. "Why don't you sit down?"

"No, thanks."

"You're afraid of me, aren't you?"

"Of course not."

He put the pipe aside. "What're you afraid of?"

"Nothing. Listen, I don't know why you're being so presumptuous," I said, "but I'm here to see the prince on business!"

"So am I. What's wrong? Think I'll sink my teeth into you? Exploit you? Treat you with disrespect?"

He was flirting with me. I decided to give in to his strange charm and flirted back. "Yes, I'm sure you're capable of all those things."

"Do you find me charming, George? I find you charming. I've heard a lot about you from Genji—"

"Really?"

"You'll come and see me sometime, won't you?"

"Why should I?"

"Because it will be a memorable experience, for both of us," he

49

replied evenly.

Prince Genji made his entrance, perfumed and decked out in colorful silks. He surveyed the situation. "WELL, I see you've made yourselves at home. Did you bring my package, T?"

Doctor T nodded, his face bland and expressionless. I could feel his eyes boring into me behind the dark sunglasses.

"And what have you brought me, George?" Genji asked.

"The first draft of the script. Is Boogie here? I'd like him to see it."

"No, he went out shopping," Genji said, with a hint of irritation. "That boy knows how to spend money—"

"She's really more than you described, Genji," Doctor T said, as if I weren't there. "Quite a young woman."

"You've always known I had good taste, T. Now, let's see what you've got," Genji said to me, putting on a pair of rose-tinted reading glasses.

I handed him the script, and he read out loud:

A poet dying in a bathtub. Smokey Robinson swaying and crooning in a blue spotlight, stage left. Women with elephant masks, stage right. A giant hypodermic needle carved out of bamboo is lowered onto this tableau. A young man dressed in a cat costume begins an electric guitar solo . . .

"WHAT'S THIS???" Prince Genji looked at me, shocked.

"Blackout," Doctor T said.

I smiled. "That's right."

"It's wonderful," Doctor T said.

Genji was unimpressed. "Wonderful? How could you say that? I can't see it."

"Well, I can." Doctor T shrugged his bony shoulders.

"And I can," I said calmly, encouraged by T's support.

"Don't you think it's a little too different? I'm not paying you to write surrealistic bullshit!" Genji exclaimed. "The public won't understand."

"I thought that's what you wanted," I said. "Our American nightmares."

"You went too **far**!"

"You're beginning to sound like a typical producer," Doctor T said. "Stop worrying about the public. I thought you were trying to be different!"

"Of course I am! BUT, I'm not too sure about that giant hypodermic needle."

Doctor T and Genji gazed at each other. Some kind of understanding passed between them.

"Well, it's your money," Genji said.

"And **yours**," Doctor T said.

"**You** seem quite taken with it."

Doctor T was casual. "I am. I have confidence in this young woman's abilities."

"I'll bet."

"Stop!!" I threw my hands up. "If you don't like it, Prince, just say so."

"My dear," Prince Genji said coolly, removing his glasses, "my co-investor in this project seems quite satisfied, so I won't argue with him—for the moment."

"I've written more, but I thought I should show you the first draft before I got too far," I said.

"**Indeed.** Well, I think I'd better dip into my vials and clear up my mind," Genji said, getting up from the sofa.

"I left the package with your butler," Doctor T said.

"Wonderful. It's been such a trying day." Genji threw his head back and looked at me. "You may leave the script here. I'll look at it again later." He walked out of the room, his scarves and scents trailing behind him.

"I don't think he likes me at all," I said. "I wonder why he even bothers . . ."

"That's not for you to worry about," Doctor T assured me. "Just remember what a rare opportunity you've stumbled into."

"Boogie got me into this. Have you met him?"

Doctor T seemed disinterested. "Yes, I have." He got up and put on his jacket. "I have to go. Would you like a ride home?"

"No, thank you."

He held out a slender, beautiful hand. "I hope to see you again."

I surprised myself with my boldness. "I'd like to go to your house instead," I said, taking his hand. He didn't say anything and led me to the driveway where his chocolate-and-creme limousine was waiting, driven by Jerome, an ageless-looking man with a basset-hound face.

The Milky Way

I could almost see my mother swoon when I called her a few days later on the telephone. "Darling," she moaned, "I've been trying to contact you for **days**! It's all over the papers—"

"**What's** all over the papers? What happened?"

"The most horrendous thing. Auntie Greta has been **murdered**."

I felt sick. "What for? Who'd want to kill him?"

"How should I know? For his antique candelabra, probably," my mother answered. "He was always courting danger, bringing home those boys he picked up on the street. He never listened to me. Maybe he was getting senile, but even after that last burglary, he kept running off to those bars as if nothing had happened."

"My god."

"It's shameful. He was brutally murdered at the age of fifty, and the police have no clues. That could've been ME!"

Dear Auntie Greta, with his crystal goblets and cheap red wine, his dapper suits, his Chihuahuas, and his vacuum cleaners. He was a sweet man, spic and span and deeply religious, confused by his deadly attraction to young, muscular boys with corrupt hearts and ethereal faces. He went to church for Sunday mass and afternoon novenas. At night, in spite of my mother's persistent nagging, he haunted the bars and the streets.

"I'm having a nervous breakdown," my mother said. "You'd better attend the memorial service. I made all the arrangements—with no help from his family, mind you."

"Aren't they coming?" I asked.

"Hell, no! They're embarrassed by all the scandal and refuse to have anything more to do with him."

"That's very kind of you. Auntie Greta would've appreciated what you're doing," I said, paying my mother a rare compliment.

She acted as if she didn't hear it. "It's just awful," she rattled on. "We aren't going to bury him in the proper way. We're having him cremated. His corpse, if you'll pardon the expression, looked so depressing I just couldn't stand it. What a nightmare!" She took a deep breath. "The memorial service is tomorrow night, and Greta's Father Confessor will officiate. All of Greta's weird friends are going to be there."

"I won't miss it," I promised, fighting back tears.

"Have you heard from your father?"

"Not lately," I said.

"Hmmm. Wonder if he's found any insects lately. Oh, well," my mother sighed, "look your best, dear. Remember, Auntie Greta would've wanted it that way."

I hung up the phone and locked myself in my studio. I refused to answer the door when Stanley knocked, demanding the rent. "Open up! I know you're home," Stanley said. "Wait till I tell Silver Daddy! He'll throw you out in the street!"

I didn't care. Finally Stanley went away, muttering loudly. I sat in the darkness for most of the night, unable to think or write, a numbness creeping over me.

At one point Silver Daddy banged on my door. "My dear, are you all right? Is there a tragedy in your family? Let me in," he begged. "I'll console you. Don't worry about the rent! I understand about the ups and downs in an artist's life. GEORGE! DON'T DO ANYTHING RASH!"

I couldn't take it anymore. Pressing my face against the door, I said as calmly as possible, "I'll be all right, Silver Daddy. **Just leave me alone.**" I was finally left in peace, tears streaming down my face.

The End of the Queen

Auntie Greta's Father Confessor led the prayers. Hundreds of people were there: hairdressers, waiters, couturiers, dancers, actors, bartenders, mimes in whiteface, aging whores, cab drivers, pharmacists, musicians, success-ful gigolos, ditchdiggers, poets and novelists, weightlifters, back-up singers in sequined dresses, sixteen-year-old basketball players in sweatpants and sneakers—and, of course, my mother.

The flowers that had been sent by Auntie Greta's numerous well-wishers and grieving cohorts glowed mystically in the semi-darkness of the chapel. The large room was stuffy with burning frankincense mixed with the scent of jasmine oil, tea rose perfume, sandalwood fans, and sweat. "I knew Auntie Greta quite well," Father Confessor began. "Are you aware that he died on the night of the full moon???" He struck a dramatic pose.

I thought it was a rather odd way to begin services for such a famous personality, especially when the entire row of poets and novelists began to snicker.

"Auntie Greta died suddenly and violently by the light of a full moon," Father Confessor continued, ignoring the poets and novelists, "and so his only heir—a ten-year-old Chihuahua named Revenge—inherited all that was left of Greta's belongings: a 9-by-12-foot frayed Persian rug and a set of gold candelabra from Barcelona, recently recovered by the police."

Father Confessor turned his gleaming eyes in my direction. "I believe your mother gave the precious candelabra to Auntie Greta during one of his frequent and suicidal bouts of depression. . . ."

A murmur went through the crowd. My mother smiled graciously as we both stood up. A spotlight came out of nowhere and beamed down on us, just like the Academy Awards on TV.

"Like mother, like daughter," my mother said, obviously delighted to be the center of attention. "As I'm always telling my daughter, 'Charity Begins at Home.' You know how these homosexuals can get despondent," she said, to my embarrassment.

The young basketball players stopped dribbling long enough to perk up their pretty puppy ears and listen.

"WELL," my mother went on, fluttering her wonderful Minnie Mouse eyelashes, "whenever Auntie Greta got sentimental, he'd always phone me to say goodbye. I'd always say, 'GOODBYE, WHAT?' And the old bag would sniff and snort and moan and announce that he was going to kill himself. I went through this melodrama with him everytime he drank. 'OH, PUH-LEEZE!' I would sigh. 'STOP FEELING SORRY FOR YOURSELF!' There's nothing quite so loathsome as self-pity, wouldn't you say?"

She directed this question at Father Confessor, who nodded solemnly.

"**Indeed,**" Father Confessor agreed, his alcoholic's face flushed and glistening with sweat, "nothing quite so loathsome."

My mother pursed her bright red lips in satisfaction. "YES, I tried to tell Auntie Greta over and over and over again—**killing yourself won't solve any of your problems**! No one cares. I mean, I care. And Auntie Greta cared. And sometimes my daughter George cares, when she isn't wrapped up with that sleazy friend of hers, Boogie, who's going to come to a bad end

too, mind you. BUT no one else cared, and Auntie Greta just wasn't being responsible. His hairdressing career was finished. Sailors mugged him constantly, and he drank too much! His liver was in shreds. In and out of the hospital he went, paying off medical bills with money he borrowed from ME. His only true friend.

"It's like I tell my daughter, 'As you get older, you'll see how lonely life really is!' Even your children turn on you," she said sweetly, giving me and the audience her most effective **Mater Dolorosa** routine.

"My daughter fancies herself an artist—a poet, to be exact. Isn't that wonderful?" my mother said. "I always encouraged her, with no help from her father. He's just an air mail letter and occasional check to her, if you know what I mean. ANYWAY, I've always believed in encouraging people to be themselves. Especially my only child, who's a poet. Or so she says. Although I try to be realistic about the situation. Like I tell her, it's okay to write all that mumbo jumbo stuff, but why not write something that makes money and save all that hocus pocus for the weekend?"

I was cringing in my seat, but I realized my mother was carried away by her own "stuff." She fanned herself grandly with a stiff palm leaf as she went on.

"Times haven't changed **that** much, and I just don't understand why my daughter's so uncooperative with me. She's always getting in and out of strange vehicles, consorting with riffraff, writing strange and confusing curses she refers to as 'poems.' Her so-called friend Boogie encourages these mystifying convolutions. I sometimes think he's also responsible for a large part of them, but I could never say that to her face.

"My daughter certainly has her pride. She wants to be given credit for everything she does. I guess she gets that from me," my mother added, smiling. "I keep warning her over and over again, just like I did Auntie Greta, about her lifestyle and her friends. Boogie's nothing but a lazy drug addict fronting himself off as a piano player. But no, she won't listen to her own mother," she said with disdain.

"**Drugs.** My daughter thinks I don't understand about the nuances of such things. She thinks I'm not **worldly**. But I've said to her often, 'There's nothing new under the sun, and you can't fool your mother!' Blood is thicker than water, and her so-called friends are going to turn on her in the end. Mark my words! I'm always right!"

The crowd held its breath in reverence and awe of her. The heat and the silence in the chapel were oppressive. We all watched in fascination as my mother swayed, her body locked into some kind of marvelous trance.

"What have I done to deserve this convolution as my child?" she asked no one in particular. "Not that I don't love her, mind you! No one knows how to love her like I do! But she doesn't understand **that**, yet. Who are these furry, dark creatures I see her mooning over? They'll never do her any good. They have no breeding! All they know how to do is make noise—and they have the nerve to call themselves **artists**! What's the world coming to, when **animals** have the arrogance to try to be like human beings, and vice versa???"

She paused, giving the mesmerized audience enough time to catch its breath.

"I don't see the order in it, do you? I'm all for affirmative action and all that sort of thing, but I can't go for these tomcats acting like they're **men**, sticking it in my daughter and her having kittens for babies. They'd end up drowned in a sack, in some canal on the south side of Chicago! And **then** what? What are those poems and so-called plays going to get her? Who would've guessed I'd have a POOR-IT for a daughter? Not a poet mind you, but a poor-it?" My mother gazed at me lovingly. "And now, my dear," she said, not missing a beat, "why don't you recite us a poem? Show us how talented you are!"

Another murmur went through the crowd. Suddenly, they all began to clap, politely at first. Then the clapping became louder and more persistent, the crowd rowdier. I was humiliated and terrified by what my mother had asked me to do.

"Tell us a poem!" the basketball players cheered.

"Tell us a poem!" the gigolos whistled.

"Yes, yes! Tell us a poem!" the hairdressers and waiters pleaded.

"Chirp it to us, sister!" the backup singers crooned.

"Tell us a poem! Show us! C'mon. Don't be an ass!" the weightlifters and cab drivers shouted, laughing and making obscene gestures.

"Whip it to us!" the poets and novelists demanded, last but not least.

Telephones began ringing as more spotlights beamed down on me. Roses showered from the ceiling, and the crowd's roaring never ceased. My mother kept bowing and blowing kisses to the grateful, bloodthirsty audience.

It was probably the grandest memorial service Auntie Greta could ever have imagined. Hysteria, melodrama, and pandemonium—Father Confessor and my mother Consuelo basking in their glory. They were oblivious to the fact that I hadn't responded to their request and was in fact heading out the door of the chapel, gritting my teeth in helpless rage. Father Confessor growled at me with some compassion, but no one else paid any attention.

"I've had it with your insults and innuendos," I said to my mother. Her eyes were shut, and she was rocking back and forth, totally unaware of my presence. "I'm sorry it had to be this way. GOODBYE."

No one tried to stop me, and I ran out of the chapel without looking back. I packed up my few belongings and took one last look at my little apartment. All in all, I had accomplished a lot of work in that cramped space. But it was time for me to move on. I owed two months' back rent, Stanley was on my case, and I couldn't stand anymore of Silver Daddy's obsequious patronage. I tiptoed down the stairs in the dead of night, past Stanley's door, and snuck out into the street. Standing on the corner, I took a deep breath and savored the growing excitement in the pit of my stomach.

I had made my decision, and I felt quite adult about it. I was moving in with Doctor T, in his gloomy mansion up in the hills.

Toots Suite

The beginning of my relationship with T was the end of my relationship with the elusive Rover, who had fled to the mountains of northern California with his guitar. Occasionally he'd send me packages of vitamins—A, B, and C—plus shark liver oil, cod liver oil, avocado cream, and placenta cream. He worried about my health and wrote me righteous little notes:

> George—
>
> I know you're living with
> a gangster. Don't be led around
> by your nose. Eat right and keep fit.
> I'm watching you.
>
> Love,
>
> Rover

"You don't need that kind of love," Doctor T would say, stuffing my nose with snowflakes. "If love were ever really love that way . . . he's just a dream. A furry face in the night. A kid who doesn't know how to fuck. Where is he when you need him, I'd like to know???" Doctor T was a master at raising doubts and suspicions.

Rover wrote me again:

> **Up above the world you fly,**
> **like a tea tray in the sky.**
> **Who's that gangster in the hat?**
> **Makin' like a superstar . . .**
> **ruining your life and looks,**
> **when you should be writing books!**

I wrote him back:

> . . . None of what you say is true. I've never been more productive.

I led a slow, leisurely life in Doctor T's mansion. Jerome, T's valet–chauffeur and trusted assistant, watched over me like an unassuming hawk. He had a subtle way about him of being in a room and watching you carefully, yet never making you feel that anything was out of the ordinary. I suppose that was his greatest talent. After a few weeks in his constant, low-key company, I even started to like him.

"Jerome is one of the only people I trust," Doctor T said. "He doesn't just work for me. He's also a friend and an assistant in all my serious under-takings. Do you understand? Don't let that doggish manner fool you. Jerome is no basset hound."

In many ways, I sought Jerome's silent approval. When I got dressed to go out, I always made sure Jerome saw what I was wearing. If he didn't say anything, that meant everything was all right. If he cleared his throat or rolled his eyes, I knew I was in trouble.

The more dependent I became, the better T liked it. "We're looking out for your interests, George. And sometimes the truth is so plain you can't even see it. Don't worry about anything—we'll take care of it."

Jerome brought in some coke, arranged it on the table, and left the room. He never got high with us. I used to wonder if he were secretly con-temptuous of my drug-ridden relationship with Doctor T.

"Stop frowning, George," Doctor T chided me, as he helped himself to some lines. "It doesn't suit you."

"I was just thinking."

"About what?"

"Jerome. What goes on inside his head."

"They call him The Roamer, George. That's all you need to know."

"Jerome The Roamer."

"Yeah, that's right."

The Doctor's imagination had no end. After we got high, he'd do it to me in the hallway, sitting on a chair, in the garden, in front of mirrors, with or without music, on the kitchen table, on the kitchen floor, in the bathtub, in the shower, in front of a movie camera, with a tape recorder running, in the morning, in the afternoon, in the evening, in the sleek slick-dick car, and with Jerome watching. Once, we even pretended to be ordinary people and got on a Greyhound bus bound for New York City. Doctor T stared out the window casually, wearing his trademark sinister sunglasses. I put my head in his lap and pretended to fall asleep, giving him the best blowjob imaginable. The thrill was unforgettable.

Sexuality replaced writing in my life. Like Doctor T, I became a master of erotic ease.

Once in a while I'd phone Prince Genji and say I was busy doing "research" for the musical.

"I'll bet," the prince would retort, knowing better. My excuses were getting weaker, and the prince was getting more hostile. One day, while T was napping, I asked Jerome to drive me to Genji's flat so I could visit Boogie.

"Where is my musical?" the prince demanded. "Am I supporting a couple of parasites? I can't keep paying all these bills and have nothing in return! All I've seen so far are notes and poems that mean nothing to me. **Nothing,**" he repeated emphatically, glaring at me with his beautiful black eyes. "I can't go to Broadway with a bunch of poems in my hand! I've got to show them something new! Something innovative! Something that's gonna make money!"

The prince turned to Boogie, who was sitting across the room, his eyes downcast. I was worried about him. I hadn't seen Boogie in weeks, and he looked smaller and thinner than I remembered. His skin had a jaundiced tinge to it.

Genji pointed a finger dramatically at Boogie. "AND YOU! Boogie, Mr. Boogie Man, where is my music? I haven't heard you play the piano in ages! I clothe you, I feed you, I fuck you when you're lonely and play host to your shady friends, but what do I get in return??? I should've known better! I never should've listened to Cinderella!" The prince was so furious, he practically pulled out his hair.

Boogie remained silent, and I was shocked by his passive response. How could he let the prince insult him? It was disgusting.

I got up from my chair and nodded to Jerome. "Let's go, Jerome. **I've had enough**," I said, sharply. I glared back at the prince. Now that I was associated with Doctor T, Genji knew better than to fuck with me. "Why don't you calm down?" I said to him. "You might develop ulcers, with all that hollerin' you do."

Boogie lifted up his head and smiled at me wanly. "Are you going so soon, George?" he asked, wistfully. I took his cold hand as he followed us like a lost orphan to the front door.

"You mustn't let that fool treat you like shit! Why do you do this to yourself?" I said, squeezing his hand. I threw my arms around Boogie. I hated to see him like this. I wanted to give him some warmth.

He quickly disentangled his frail body from my embrace. He was still wearing that vacuous smile.

"Oh, George, the prince is right. I'm full of shit. I'm living off him, and I don't do anything to earn my keep."

"I'm sure you've done your share," I said. "At any rate, we're not under contract to him, you know! Nothing says we **have** to produce. Why don't you pack your stuff and come with me?"

Jerome looked askance in my direction, but I ignored him. "C'mon, Boogie. You need to get away from this dungeon."

Boogie shook his head. "No. Not today. I'm not ready yet. In spite of what you think or say, I owe Genji **something**. If it weren't for him, I'd be nobody. I'm glad you're safe and happy. As for me, I've got accounts to settle."

I kissed him on the cheek. "I'll call you in a few days."

Safe and happy, indeed! If only Boogie knew the truth, I thought, as Jerome drove up Doctor T's long and winding driveway. T was standing on the front steps, wearing one of his caftans. I knew he was naked underneath.

"Where have the two of you been?" he wanted to know. "I was getting worried."

"She asked me to drive her to Genji's," Jerome said, deadpan. "Genji pulled another one of his famous scenes and treated us **rudely**. Something should be done about that madman."

The Doctor took me in his arms, and I snuggled up to him wearily. He nibbled softly on my ears. "Did Genji treat you rudely, my dear? Are you upset?"

I nodded.

"Oh my, I guess we'll have to do something about that, won't we?" T murmured. He led me into the house and up into the bedroom.

I got in bed and crawled under the covers. "T, I'm worried about Boogie."

T had his back to me as he sat on the edge of the bed, mixing some new concoction for us to snort. "What is it, darling? Has the prince turned your friend into a junkie?"

"I get the feeling you don't think much of Boogie."

"He's frivolous," T said, grinning. Even when he grinned, there was a coldness in his eyes that unnerved me. He had asked nothing of me in the beginning, only that I sit back and enjoy the luxuries he had to offer, give him the benefit of a doubt, and snort up to my heart's content. When he started feeling rushes of paranoia, he asked me to stay up all night and play dominoes with him. I was the better domino player, and the most "intelligent" fuck (as he put it) he had ever had. He even asked me to read my poems and stories to him before we went to bed—a vulnerable, whimsical side of his personality no one else was allowed to see. Not even the trusted Jerome.

It was easy for me to love Doctor T, but I couldn't understand how he could be so cruel about my only friend. It was a source of constant friction between us.

"Why do you call him a junkie?" I asked. "What's the difference between him and us?"

"What do you mean by that question, George?" T handed me the dope.

"Well, here **you** are, turning me on to this and that, while Genji turns Boogie on to that and this. What's the difference?"

"The difference, George, is in the **quality** of this and that. I'm afraid your friend is off into the deep end."

I was horrified. "You mean needles and heroin and all that sort of thing?"

T said nothing.

"I still don't understand," I blithered, "the difference between him and us. I mean, I'm just as strung out on you, aren't I?"

In fact, the Doctor's detachment was making me horny. Or was it because I was high? I didn't care anymore. The hell with Rover, who was just another memory! The hell with art!

T looked pained. "You ask too many questions, George. Sometimes I just can't deal with your questions. What do you want of me? Don't I love you enough?"

I couldn't stand to see him upset. Gazing into his snakelike eyes, hypnotized and loving it all the way, I licked the center of the palms of his hands, very slowly, the way the Beast licked water from Beauty's hands in the 1939 movie I once saw and never forgot.

"Of course you love me," I whispered, higher than a kite, higher than a rocket on its way to the moon, higher than anyone could be if they'd just finished a musical. . . .

It was Boogie who said that the trouble with us was we weren't even niggers. "I mean, what are we selling, and who wants to hear it?" he'd say, his wasted eyes skimming over my halfhearted attempts at a script. "They already got niggers to entertain them. What's so interesting about us?"

I didn't understand him, but what he said disturbed me deeply. I knew Boogie was seeing something clear and terrifying, that summer of splendor in Genji's gothic palace.

The prince was pressuring Boogie tremendously, tired of having Boogie on the payroll, perhaps even tired of Boogie himself. Boogie had nowhere else to go, no other piano to play. Off to Doctor T's house he would run, seeking whatever kind of solace I could offer him. He wouldn't leave Genji's place until it was dark, claiming the glaring sunlight hurt his eyes.

"I'm okay," Boogie would grin, seeing the worried look on my face.

T put up with Boogie only because I demanded it of him, and Boogie was sensitive to this. It made for long and uncomfortable silences whenever T came into the room, which he often did just to intimidate Boogie.

I made Boogie cup after cup of Constant Comment tea sweetened with honey. I forced him to eat the gourmet hot links T would grill on Saturday nights. We sat down to awkward, formal dinners set by fussy Jerome with candles and fresh flowers, eating our hot links smeared with Dijon mustard and sipping Dom Perignon champagne.

I dragged Boogie to the movies with us, but more often than not Boogie nodded out through most full-length features. The only movies he'd stay awake for were cartoons. Bugs Bunny made him crack up hysterically whenever he said, "What's up, **Doc**?"

As a musical team, we felt abandoned. Toyed with and cast aside. In desperation I clung to my romantic fantasy with Doctor T. Boogie, on the other hand, clung to me.

One night, very late, when Doctor T and Jerome were out making one of their sinister "deliveries," Rover phoned. It was one of the few times T had left me alone. I was nervous and jumpy, knowing he was capable of slithering into the bedroom at any moment.

"Are you all right?" Rover asked, in his most official tone of voice.

In his inimitable, feline way, he sensed something was wrong. That made me feel better, somehow.

"No, I'm not," I said, staring absent-mindedly at the ceiling. Cobwebs formed lacey patterns on the antique chandelier. "How'd you get this number, Rover? It's unlisted."

"I have my sources, too, you know! What about this hoodlum you're living with? Does your mama know about him?"

"I'm old enough to do as I please," I retorted, highly insulted. "She doesn't know where I am, in answer to your question."

"A girl of your breeding should know better," Rover said. "You know, your breeding is what attracted me to you in the first place. Plus your latent talents. I thought you'd be different from all the other bitches, if you'll excuse the expression."

"That's just too bad, isn't it! I didn't measure up to **your** high expectations!"

"I know what's happening with you, George. That's why I left town. I've retreated to my hideout in the mountains, where the stars are real and gangsters are something you read about in the papers."

"Stop calling him a gangster."

"Face it, George—that's no doctor! And he doesn't have long to live," Rover said, ominously. "He's too upwardly mobile for his own good—and he isn't as slick as he thinks he is. I've heard all about it, on the subterranean grapevine. He's got people out looking for him, George. **Watch out.**"

Abruptly, he hung up.

T was mad, of that I was quite sure. He slept with a gun by our bed. Sometimes I'd wake in the night to find him padding softly around the house with a flashlight, checking all the doors and windows, making sure everything was locked up tight.

"You never know," he'd say, when I asked why he was so paranoid.

He professed disdain for people who used needles, but he'd recently acquired a new habit—furtively shooting up coke when he thought I was asleep. He locked himself up in the little room next to the kitchen that he referred to as his "sanctuary." Jerome and I weren't allowed in that room without his permission. When they were out on "business," the room was padlocked.

T would say, with a sad smile, "A lot of people don't like me, George. You know that, don't you?"

I agreed with everything he said. It was less trouble, and it seemed to take so little to appease him—in the beginning.

Jerome placated him by being available for T's every whim and desire: long, aimless drives by the ocean or trips to the movies at the spur of the moment. Doctor T had no other way of relating to the world. He enjoyed sitting in a dark theater with crowds of teenagers hooting at the screen. It made him feel "alive," and yet above it all. Otherwise, he would go into a rage and lock himself in the little room for days. All we could hear were groans and the sounds of objects being thrown around in a fury.

Soon after these increasing fits of lunacy began, I realized that I was practically a prisoner in this mansion. The ever-faithful Jerome had been assigned to keep an even more watchful eye over me and monitor all my phone calls.

T accused me of knowing too much. He kept a tight and painful grip on my arms and shook me like a ragdoll. "Who told you people were after me?" he demanded. **"How did you know?"**

"No one. No one told me anything. I never said that!"

I watched as he switched on the flashlight and looked under the bed. "What are you doing, T? This isn't necessary."

"You don't know about these things," he muttered. "Your name isn't on a list."

"**What** list? Come on, T, let's go to bed. You haven't been to sleep in days. You need rest."

"Ah, George. You care about me, don't you? Yes, I know that about you. We're like two guitars in love—so in tune with each other. Don't ever leave me, George."

"I'm here, T. You don't have to worry. Get some rest. I'll watch the house," I said.

T suddenly laughed. "You bitch! I know what you've got on your mind! Slip me a few downers so I pass out. Then you can climb out the window and meet that pussy friend of yours—what's-his-name, Rover The Cat! Or maybe it'll be that faggot Boogie who's been dying to fuck you for years. Yeah, that's right. He's been masquerading as a faggot. MY GOD! I NEVER THOUGHT OF IT BEFORE! OF COURSE! THE PERFECT COVER-UP!"

He went on ranting and raving, gripping me tightly and bringing tears to my eyes. When he saw my tears, he would stop and hold me close to him, stroking my hair. "I'm sorry, baby love. Be patient. I'm going out of it again."

I wasn't really afraid of him then. It was just so awful to see him fall apart. Usually Jerome would come in the room and discreetly rescue me from further harassment by distracting T with business suggestions or offers to go to nightclubs or the movies. As T became crazier, however, he shunned public places. Even Jerome became subject to T's suspicions. He accused us of conspiring against him.

"I know Jerome wants to fuck you," T would say, his eyes gleaming like a wolf's in the dark.

How wild he looked, and yet I loved him even in his delirium and wanted only to make him better. I told him over and over I loved him and held him like a child. We would cry and make promises to each other, then end up fucking so passionately I'd get dizzy with his smell, the feel of his tongue licking the salt on my skin. When he wearied of me, finally, he would drift off into a nervous sleep.

One night he sat up with a jolt on the bed. I could feel his eyes on me, but I kept my breathing steady and pretended to be fast asleep. He turned the flashlight on my face, whispering, "Are you under the bed, George? **Are you under the bed?**"

Occasionally I phoned my mother. She always went into hysterics at the sound of my voice. "Is it you? Is it really you? Oh god, I've got the police out looking for you."

"Good grief, Mama."

"Where did you run off to after Auntie Greta's memorial service? Where are you staying now? Are all those rumors true? **GEORGE,** if you don't tell me the truth, I'm going to write your father a nasty letter."

"It's okay, Mama. I already wrote him a letter telling him not to worry. It's exactly what he wants to hear," I said.

"GEORGE! Don't think you can go on like this forever! How can you do this to me? I'm having a nervous breakdown!"

After a few more of the same kind of conversations, I stopped trying to talk to my mother at all. T became the center of my life. Whatever I wanted, he gave me—except the freedom to come and go as I pleased. At first, he was so fascinating and consuming that I really didn't mind. He never bothered me when I wrote, and I was even close to finishing the script for Prince Genji. Only when he interfered with my friendship with Boogie did I realize that things had gotten out of hand.

"I don't like the way he looks," T said. "I never liked junkies. They're disgusting."

I'd had enough of his righteousness. "And what do you call yourself? I know you're shooting up in that room when I'm asleep," I blurted out.

I knew I'd gone too far, as soon as I said it. Jerome wasn't home, and I had no one to defend me.

T stared at me for a moment with astonishment. "How wonderful you are, George. How you amaze me, with your perception. Darling, darling! How did you guess?"

He began slapping me around my head and my face. As I tried moving away from him, he hit me anywhere he could—on my sides, on my belly, on the arms I threw up to protect my face.

"STOP IT!" I gasped. "STOP IT!" I was screaming and crying, but it didn't matter to Doctor T anymore.

I loved him, and I couldn't understand why. He was a frenzied animal, and he just kept on hurting me.

Rice Congee:
Dubious Treasures

I was a mess. I hadn't been sleeping or eating, keeping up with T's hallucinations. After he beat me, he fell on his knees and wept, begging my forgiveness. Then he ordered Jerome to drive me to the hospital. They treated my bruises and didn't ask any questions.

I stayed in bed for days, reading comic books and scribbling in my journal. My condition seemed to take T's mind off his paranoia. He seemed like his old solicitous self, serving me meals in bed and encouraging me to finish the play. He got me high when I complained about my aches and pains. I remember giggling with him about it, and trying to fuck afterwards—except everything hurt too much, and I went to sleep instead.

I thought the nightmare was over. I finished the play and convinced myself that T was under a lot of pressure and consequently had "overreacted" when he beat me. I didn't want to think about it anymore. I wanted to go on living my fairytale life, lying to myself about the perverseness of my relationship.

T was giving me a sponge bath with scented water when the invitation to Boogie's party arrived, via Jerome.

I glanced nervously at T.

"Open it," he smiled. "I know you miss him."

I tore open the envelope. "Oh, T!" I squealed. "It's Boogie's birthday, and he wants to celebrate my finishing the play!"

"How delightful. Isn't that delightful, Jerome?" T said. "Maybe the boy's straightening out."

Jerome was silent. T dried me with a towel. "Well, baby, do you want me to go?" T asked, caressing me with his voice.

"Of course I do! And you too, Jerome!" I said, throwing my arms around T.

I couldn't believe the sudden turn of events. Maybe everything was going to be all right, after all.

This was no ordinary birthday party, and I worried about what to give Boogie as a present. I had written him a poem, but was dissatisfied with it:

> **dying fawn**
> **sun of anubis**
> **yr corrupt song**
> **is choreographed**
> **by the supremes**

the white bandit
holds you by the neck
on a diamond-studded leash
or is it the silver conch belt
of jimi's corpse?

"How morbid," Jerome said, after reading it.

I thought Jerome had impeccable taste, so I asked him if he would go shopping for me. "Pick out a piece of jewelry for Boogie—a bracelet, a necklace, anything. I'll give it to him with the poem."

Jerome left that afternoon to go shopping. T had been in his little sanctuary all day, but I wasn't worried. He even had the door unlocked.

At T's request, Genji had brought me back a formal silk kimono from Japan. I tried it on in front of the mirror, wondering if it was too outlandish to wear to the party. As I stared at my reflection, T suddenly appeared behind me. Electric Miles Davis was playing on the stereo, and T danced around to the dense and sinister rhythms.

He thrust his pelvis in my direction, stepping here and there, snapping his fingers and moving his head from side to side.

"Feel good, don'tcha?" He leered.

I tried to kiss him, but he avoided me. Thinking this was a new game, I grabbed his arm. He giggled, pushing me away.

"What're you up to?" I asked, confused.

"Feel good, don'tcha?" he repeated, whirling around the room. He danced up close to me and stuck his pretty tongue out, in a pose that would've lit up Broadway.

"Yeah, I feel good," I said, leaning up toward his face for a kiss. He spit at me instead.

I was stunned. For a long while I just stood there, not sure it had really happened until I felt his saliva dripping down my cheek.

He grinned. "Feel good, don'tcha" He spit on me again.

I backed out of the room, slowly.

"WHERE DO YOU THINK YOU'RE GOING? Don't you want a kiss? I thought you wanted a kiss—"

"You're crazy."

"Yes, George! That's what they say," T sang, in a falsetto reminiscent of all that was good about Detroit.

"You've been shooting up again."

"Yes, George! You're absolutely right!" T agreed, coming at me.

I ran out of the room, but he caught up with me in the hallway and pushed me up against the wall. "Don't worry about your friend, George," he said, panting heavily. "I've got a nice present for him, and we're all going to have a good time."

"I'm not going with you," I said.

He laughed. "That's too bad, isn't it? You have no choice, George. You have no choice. . . ."

Silver Daddy was there—and Tinkerbelle, smoking her inevitable Gauloise. Porno wore a lavender jumpsuit and pink dancer's legwarmers. Momma Magenta was carrying a sketchpad and her black portfolio. Cinderella stood demurely in the shadows, a corsage of gardenias on her wrist and a shimmering gold net veil masking her face.

"Are you all right?" Momma Magenta asked me, looking concerned.

I nodded, avoiding her eyes. T had a grip on my arm, and I didn't want to cause a scene.

The living room was lavishly decorated for the party. Prince Genji was busy lighting the candles on Boogie's piano-shaped birthday cake. Jerome was standing next to him.

"Jerome!" I called out. "Did you get the present for Boogie?"

He looked uncomfortable as T answered for him. "Of course he did, darling. Jerome's a responsible man."

"What did you end up getting him?" I asked Jerome, trying to ignore T.

Jerome shrugged his shoulders. "I'm not sure," he stammered. "T had it all wrapped up. I didn't even have to go shopping. As a matter of fact, I just gave it to Boogie."

"The present's from you and me, darling," T said.

I looked around the room for my friend. "Where is he?" I asked Genji.

"How should I know? That boy's so irresponsible."

Porno pulled an ivory comb out of her silk purse and began combing her hair. "Yes, he is rather irresponsible, isn't he?" she agreed.

"How do you know? You've never even met him!" I said to her, annoyed.

"He should never have gotten into buggery so young," Silver Daddy intoned, sipping the **sake** the tuxedo-clad butler poured him.

"I don't think we should be criticizing him at his own party," I grumbled, freeing my arm from T's viselike grip. He was too busy whispering into Porno's ear to notice what I'd done.

"Well, if he doesn't show up soon, I shall blow out his candles for him!" Porno declared, licking her glossy red lips. She fluttered her lashes at me. "George, you look different. Are you well? Did you ever finish your project? I must tell you about my latest movie. You'd love it."

I ignored her narcissistic blitherings.

"Where's Boogie?" I repeated, for the benefit of everyone in the room.

They stared at me as if I were crazy. Then the chattering resumed.

"Have some wine," Prince Genji said.

I looked at him blankly. "It's his birthday party, and he should be here,"

I insisted. "Don't you think it's a little strange?"

"Your hair wants cutting," Tinkerbelle said to me suddenly.

"You should learn not to make such personal remarks," Silver Daddy reprimanded her. "It's very rude."

He turned to the rest of us. "Why is a raven like a writing-desk?"

Genji clapped his hands. "A riddle, a riddle! I love riddles! Riddles clear up the atmosphere! Riddles break the ice! This is going to be a grand party—I just know it!"

"I certainly hope so," Momma Magenta said. She pulled out her Rapidograph pen and began to draw.

Doctor T was kissing Porno's wrist, and she was blushing. Cinderella was conferring with Jerome in one corner. Porno cast a furtive glance in my direction. I grinned back at her.

"Do you know where Boogie is, Porno dear?"

"NO, I DON'T!" And I do wish you'd stop asking that question," she replied, highly agitated. She offered T her other wrist to kiss.

He began slowly sucking on her fingers, while gazing at me. I was furious.

Genji rushed over to where we sat. "T—it's so good to see you! Would you like some wine? How about some **sake**? No? Well, I've got some champagne chilling, just for you!"

I tapped Genji on the shoulder. "When was the last time you saw Boogie?"

Genji threw his arms up in exasperation. "WHO CAN REMEMBER TRIVIAL DETAILS? I'm not sure about anything, at this point!"

Jerome cleared his throat. "I believe he's taking a shower."

"A shower? It's nearly midnight," Silver Daddy remarked.

"You might just as well say 'I see what I eat' is the same thing as 'I eat what I see,'" Tinkerbelle said.

"You might just as well say 'I like what I get' is the same thing as 'I get what I like!'" Silver Daddy added, lasciviously.

"It is the same thing with you," Porno said to him, and everyone stopped talking.

At that instant, the butler Esteban broke the silence by hitting a brass gong with a large mallet. Prince Genji ushered everyone into their chairs, then clapped his hands.

"Rice congee! Rice congee!" he chirped.

"Rice congee?" Cinderella inquired, politely. It was the only thing she said all night.

"My dear, it's toothsome!" Genji assured her. "Toothsome and gratifying, in a most subtle way."

The candles were melting on Boogie's piano-shaped cake.

"But whatever is it?" Porno asked, her hand in Doctor T's lap.

"Some sort of porridge," Momma Magenta suggested.

"Some sort of stew," Tinkerbelle said, blowing Gauloise smoke in our faces.

"YOU'RE ALL WRONG, AS USUAL!" Silver Daddy proclaimed. "When I was in Asia, I had the pleasure of gormandizing rice congee **au table** each morning, in the company of defrocked Himalayan monks—"

"Not in the morning exclusively!" Genji sniffed interrupting Silver Daddy. "A true devotee of **chinoiserie de luxe** learns to ruminate rice congee morning, noon, and **apres le bain**, if you know what I mean!"

"Speaking of **apres le bain**," I began, not really wanting to interfere with this sudden flow of esoteric knowledge, "hasn't Boogie finished his bath yet?"

"There you go again," Doctor T sneered. "Why don't you relax and eat your dinner? Boogie's probably primping."

"In the old days," Silver Daddy continued, undaunted, "the women of Chinese aristocracy blended powdered pearls with their rice congee to maintain their luxurious complexions."

"You might just as well say 'You are what you eat!' " Momma Magenta chimed in.

A huge silver tureen was wheeled into the room by the butler Esteban.

Genji was ecstatic. "Hmmm . . . rice congee with eight treasures! Can anyone guess what the eight treasures are?"

"A riddle! A riddle!" Porno squirmed in her seat.

"We've always **loved** riddles," Tinkerbelle said.

Genji turned to Silver Daddy. "Well, my dear authority, can you name a treasure?"

Silver Daddy cleared his throat and stuck out his chest. "It seems to me, if I remember Kyoto correctly, rice congee contained tree fungus, rat's ears, and dried lily flowers."

"Wrong!" Genji seemed to relish embarrassing Silver Daddy. "This is rice congee with eight treasures—my custom-made concoction ordered especially from Taiwan! Jerome? What about you? Take a guess."

"I wouldn't know," Jerome said, looking terribly out of place.

"Well, then, you can't play the game, can you? PORNO, if you'd stop giving that man a handjob and give it a thought, I'm sure you can guess at least ONE of the treasures."

"BAH-NAH-NAH," Porno purred, without missing a stroke. T lay back in his chair, a dreamy look on his face.

"Excellent!" Genji beamed. "One treasure down, seven more to go! We can't eat until we solve the riddle. How about you, Momma Magenta?"

Momma Magenta dipped her pinky into the steaming tureen. "Gnats, boils, blood, death of the first-born!"

Genji slapped her wrist with a jade-encrusted fan. "**Wrong!** This isn't Passover, dear. Not the plagues of Egypt on my house!" He sighed, tiring of his own game. "**Red beans and bananas, dates, lotus nuts, chestnuts and longan, grapes, and white gourd** . . . the eight treasures in rice congee, my friends."

The fragrant rice congee was served in delicate porcelain bowls. Genji sat at the head of the table, watching his guests attack the food with immense satisfaction.

I glanced at Momma Magenta's Mickey Mouse watch. It was past midnight, and there were still no signs of the guest of honor.

I got up from the table. "I'm going to look for Boogie."

Everyone stopped eating.

"You can't do **that**," Tinkerbelle said.

"You can't do **that**," Porno agreed.

"It's rude!" Silver Daddy was offended. "**Artists may be artists**, but manners are always important!"

"She's never been too **social**," Genji said, giving demure Cinderella a meaningful look.

T ignored us all and went on eating.

"I'll go with you," Jerome said suddenly. I was taken aback by the kindness in his voice but didn't say anything. We left the room and started up the winding stairs toward the bedrooms.

"I'm not sure," Jerome said, "but I think this has something to do with that present I brought him."

"**What** present? You mean what T gave you? Why didn't you bring him my poem? Why didn't you buy him a bracelet, like I said? WHAT HAVE YOU DONE?"

"I'm guilty of a lot of things, but I'm not a **killer**."

I was horrified. "What was in that package, Jerome? Don't you know?"

He avoided my eyes. "I thought you were in on it."

I ran down the hall, opening doors to bedrooms and closets, frantically searching for my friend. Towels and sheets fell on me, Siamese cats meowed and hissed as I ran in and out of rooms. Genji's caged jungle birds were in an uproar, flapping their wings and shrieking. They seemed to sense my mounting panic. I was dizzy with the heavy odor of incense perfume, thrown off guard by the numerous mirrors reflecting my every move.

Nearing the sound of water running, I walked slowly in the direction of Genji's bathroom. I motioned to Jerome. "Come with me," I said. "I don't want to go in there alone."

The door to the bathroom was ajar. The sound of running water was deafening to my ears. I worked up my nerve and pushed open the door, Jerome hovering anxiously behind me. We were unable to see at first because of the steam, but it soon became all too clear. Boogie lay crumpled up in the shower—his face blue and serene, the remains of a mighty fix scattered on the floor around him, blood and water flowing down the drain.

Roller-Skating on Saturn's Rings

Everyone, of course, had an alibi: They were downstairs in Prince Genji's dining room having rice congee for dinner.

"**Heroin?** My goodness! We never touch the stuff!" Prince Genji said to the lieutenant who was interrogating us.

After the police finished asking their questions, the ambulance came and took the corpse away. T and I got into the limosine. He wanted to take Porno home with us, but I slammed the car door in her face. T never said a word.

Jerome drove us home. We were suffering from exhaustion and a vague uneasiness with each other that was new and unsettling. As soon as we arrived at the mansion, T locked himself in his little room. I laid on our bed and wept.

Jerome came into the bedroom, nattily dressed in a navy blue pinstriped suit. "I've packed my bags and given notice," he said. "I can't stay here any longer."

I felt extraordinarily calm. "Where are you going?"

"Hollywood. Maybe I'll go into the music business."

"Don't be too hard on yourself."

"It's true, isn't it? I'm just a glorified gopher." He lowered his voice. "Do you want to come? He's locked up in that room again."

"Don't worry about me. I'm not afraid of him anymore."

"I'll leave the front door unlocked." He blew me a gentle kiss and left.

It was still dark outside. I hadn't turned on the lights in the house, or the heat. I stayed, sitting on the bed, shivering and numb with grief. The phone rang.

"It's me," Rover said.

I was so weary I could barely talk. "**YOU.** Is it, really?"

"Yup. It's me—with some news for you. A few minutes ago, Genji's place went up in flames. Some say it was arson. Nothing remains."

"I'm sure it was arson, and I'm sure it was committed by a ghost," I said.

"They're coming to take the gangster away. He can't pull this one off and get away with it."

"I know."

"Well, what're you gonna do? Who's gonna take care of you now?"

"I'll take care of myself."

"Do you love him?"

"Yes."

"**GEORGE,** you've blown it again!"

It was my turn to hang up.

I decided not to take anything with me except my notebooks and one or two drawings. I left the manuscript on the bed.

The night was stunningly beautiful, with a full, orange moon—a painted backdrop on the set of an innocent movie where all you had to do was dance a watered-down version of the rhumba and sing Cole Porter tunes to be happy, accepted, and free.

T was standing on the balcony. He howled at the moon, reaching out with his slender arms as if the moon were his to possess.

"How lovely you look," I said, knowing he would still be there when the sun came up, knowing he couldn't see me.

My bones ached, and I felt a sudden rush as I walked down the street.

It was always that way with me when it was time for me to go.

The Woman Who Thought She Was More Than a Samba

the woman who thought
she was more than a samba
rode underground trains
dressed up for dancing,
as usual

never mind
that she looked good
succulent like peaches
tattoos on her skin
enough to make
most men sigh

rats
strung out on methadone
rode underground trains
with her,
rats in a trance
scratching
balancing oblivious children
on their laps

rats in a trance
scratching
asleep
ears glued
to radios blaring
city music
metallic abrasive
hard city music

the woman who thought
she was more than a samba
rode underground trains
terrified
she'd forget
how to dance

her dreams
were filled with ghosts
young men she knew

who danced
with each other
consumed by
ambiguous dilemmas

grinding their narrow hips
to snakelike city music
metallic abrasive hard city music
grinding their narrow hips
against her sloping,
naked back
like buffalos
shedding their fur
against a tree
whispering—"it's a shame
you aren't a man . . .
you have so much man
in you"

in brazil
the women samba
only with their legs
their faces are somber
and their upper torsos
never move

in haiti
people draw themselves
without arms
and don't seem
to dance at all

exuding matinee idol ambience
the young men she knew
wore white
and sported moustaches
"we are a tropical people"
they reminded her,
"the most innovative
in the universe"
they gyrated desperately
and stayed drunk in bars
"we're **in**, this year"

it's a shame
i weren't a man

and who's the woman here?
she often asked herself
sometimes she screamed:
i'm older than you think
i'm getting so sick of you
i can't even remember your names
you all look the same . . .

she fell in love once
and the wounds never healed
it was romance
old as the hills
predictable in its maze
what medieval tapestry he wove
to keep her still

gazelles loped
past their window
and veils kept out the sun
she had her own take on things,
her perfume-scented version
of the story
never mind that
he always won,
leaving unfinished poems
under her bed
orchestras strung upside-down
from the ceiling
traces of blood as souvenirs
of their exclusive
combat zone

the woman who thought
she was more than a samba
carried her solitude around
in pouches made of chinese silk
changing her jewelry
with each new lover
insisting they move
with sullen grace
stressing the importance
of style
on a dance floor
how arrogantly they might
hold up
their leonine heads

on a dance floor
how arrogantly they might
hold up
their leonine heads

her dreams were filled with ghosts
perched on her bony wrists
grinning gargoyles
who menaced her every step
and wouldn't
let her go

she longed to be
her mother
in a silver dress
some softly fading memory
lifting her legs
in a sinuous tango

I Went All the Way Out Here Looking for You, Bob Marley

but you left this island
of bananas and poinsettias
i imagined was so much
like my own
how could you leave
before my arrival
you must've known
your songs got the same
english madness
i got stuck with

and here i am
spending christmas
in your country
and you aren't even here
and these lovely women
drive us around
to dull intellectual parties
just like california
and i ask about you
cuz i figure
there are some very influential types
present
and they must know
your phone number and address
possibly even arrange
the grand rendezvous
of all times

but as soon as i mention
your name
they smile and shake their heads
"no, he's not here," they say
"he left the country. . ."

and my friend suggests
taking a plane to your new house
i mean after all
we came all the way out here
to have this conversation and dance
with you

78

but the intellectuals
shake their heads and are bemused
"he lives somewhere
between the bahamas and london . . ."
then they say
"sometimes he visits new york"

the bahamas'is okay with me
but london is incapable
of exciting my imagination
and i know your mama
lives in new jersey
or wilmington delaware
or maybe miami
but i don't see you
walkin' down eighth street
in the snow
or emerging from
abyssmal subway stations
my own extraterrestrial
prehistoric futuristic
man

how could you do this to me
there are so many questions
i need to ask you
like who "they" and "them" are
everybody in your country
keeps talkin' about

are they horsemen of darkness
descending from blue mountains
in the middle of the night
or malevolent spirits
cutting open children's vaginas
to facilitate rape
because children don't align themselves
with the right party

and who are they
laying there with balls cut off
because they don't belong
to anything
and do women fear
walking home
and who are they
blocking the streets

with all this music
telling me about them
who drive me around
in their cars
and instigate terror
with their theories

all i know is
them don't got your records
in their houses
and they don't live
in the hills
and them are genteel
and offer me homemade sorrel brew
and pimento liqueurs
and peacocks are caged
in their gardens
and they don't speak english too well
and them can read
and they can't
and them can write
and they can't
and them work
and they don't
and them are leaving the country
in droves
and they can't or won't

and this just isn't fair
because you are the only one
i trust
i have to know
were you shot in the arm
like they said
and don't they know
they can't kill music like that?

they should take heed
from america
and relegate you to the
sheraton hotel's junkanoo lounge
as a malnourished dance band

and this just isn't fair
because you are the only one
i trust
and i haven't even met you yet
and i am
waiting   —Kingston, Jamaica, 1977

80

Chiqui and Terra Nova

such a strange girl / chiquita / hangin' out with the likes of terra nova / a
man / woman / what polite people refer to as transvestite / terra
nova / bundled up in technicolor crocheted doily shirts / outdated sixties'
bellbottoms / dressed in the outdated chic / of rock stars' old ladies / like
chiquita remembered seein' / in the backstages of fillmore east and
fillmore west / when jimi hendrix was still alive / some shy young man
with blown-out hair everyone ignored / in those days

but jimi was dead / and terra nova reigned / in the streets of new
york city / carrying her bundle of technicolor clothes and opalescent
jewelry / new york city / the only city that mattered / in terra nova's
serene opinion

"it's not as if i haven't traveled" / she would say / "it's not as if i
haven't been to kansas–st. louis missouri–grand rapids michigan–new
jersey–or cicero illinois . . . i've even given california a whirl . . . some old
man took me to paris for a one-night stand near the folies bergere! but i
couldn't stay . . . everything was too historical and they kept egypt locked
up in some museum basement . . . san francisco's too slow for
me . . . oakland too much to handle . . . los angeles far too spatial! i like to
walk at night . . . but l.a. cops are trigger-happy in the wrong way . . ."

and terra nova would flash her famous smile / at chiquita / who she
now accepted as a friend / after all / it was chiqui who named this
spirit / new earth / a found poem / in rags / they haunted
streets / together / sometimes peering into cars / parked along the
river / in the late night / watching men / jack off men / languidly /
nervously / or desperately

but **jimi was dead** and what about transsexuals? chiqui often asked
her friend / terra nova was proud of the fact that she was not one / or
the other

"i hesitate to speak on the subject" / terra nova replied / "only
because one never knows, one never knows. . ." like the weather / one of
terra nova's favorite subjects

chiqui and terra nova would lean against a car / parked on
christopher street in the early morning / and discuss last night's t.v.
news / terra nova had a crush on ed bradley / and was a fan of CBS / "he
seems so kind and unapproachable / **a real man**" / she would sigh / but
it was the weather report that infuriated her / snide and smug
weathermen and women who predicted sunshine / five days in advance

"how could they know?" / terra nova cried / **"how could they know!**
and how dare they disturb my atmosphere with BAD NEWS" / BAD

NEWS / terra nova had no room for that / in her life

and whenever chiqui asked about transsexuals / which she often did / bein' a young and fascinated woman / curious about silicone breasts / artificial vaginas / and stitched-on penises / terra nova would refer to one of her cherished movies / "frankenstein" / any version would do

"now / you think about that / GIRL / you think about that" / was all terra nova murmured closing large almond-shaped eyes and nodding her head slowly / her dishevelled mass of curls / shaking this way / and that / how melancholy overcame her as she marvelled at the world and **jimi hendrix dead** so many years

once / when chiqui had some money / she bought terra nova a new wig / a royal peacock blue wig / and terra nova threw back her head and laughed and laughed and embraced the smiling chiquita / "my chiquita banana" / terra nova crooned

terra nova wore her new electric blue wig to washington square park and danced for a giggling crowd / sang stevie wonder songs out-of-tune / but didn't care / was joyful even when the rain came down and the crowd dispersed

chiqui and terra nova collected more quarters and dimes than any hustler in the park that afternoon / strolling down the streets arm-in-arm / like tropical apparitions / only visible to a few

Yolanda Meets the Wild Boys

After the paradiso and the milky way and the kosmos, seeming
as if we had all been sent to gig at some celestial city—
which, despite what some folks think, AMSTERDAM IZ NOT—we
strolled along some canal in the late night in search of that
nebulous JAZZ which might be happening in a garage
masquerading as a nightclub. I turned to lorenzo and said
(—or was it lewis? we were all walking together stoned and
speeding and exhausted)
                        "Shit—this is almost as bad as the
jazz life . . ."
                what david murray refers to as the jazz life
y'know . . . and I **should** know, all of us here
like grinning creatures of the underworld,
poeticizing to young zombies asleep in the deep hashish maze
of netherlands bliss, borrowing from katmandu and goa,
in love with japanese hair, the waterfalls of africa
and what would my mother say if she knew? That i
shoulda had a job, vuitton luggage, a bathtub
in the george cinq hotel.
        Not this yolanda, screeching back to the wild boys
of romance, wild boys lurking in the shadows of the grimy
paradiso balcony, wild boys chanting "BULLSHIT BULLSHIT"
to all the weary poets, while yolanda yells back
                        "fuckyoutoo,jack!"
tensely awaiting a confrontation that does not come.
        THE YOUNG PUNKS OF AMSTERDAM play follow-the-leader,
coming alive only when their band appears. They grab each other's
crotches, and it's an all-male show, the women highly made-up and
strangely passive. I'm feeling too old for this and don't believe much of
what i see: wearing black, young blond boys writhe around the stage floor
deliriously anti-rhythmic at the feet of their rock n'roll idol, who leaps
about and throws his hips in their faces.
                "HEY THERE MUTHAFUCKAS
            I'LL SHOW YOU SOME REAL ROCK N'ROLL!"
yolanda sings in english.
        The boys don't seem to care or understand. They want their
band! She pulls out
her folsom st. whip and whirls the silver microphone above
her head, like a space-age cowgirl in a rodent rodeo.

"SAY BOYS, CAN YA ONLY GET IT UP
        FOR EACH OTHER?" yolanda teases, rolling her eyes
and cracking her black whip. "HERE'S SOME REAL BLACK
                    FOR YA—some san francisco
        boys' town action!   The crowd is transfixed
as yolanda slashes the whip across their idol's back,
ripping off his t-shirt and drawing blood.
            "YOLANDA WANTS TO KNOW—can you
                handle it, or are we merely playing?" she grins.

        They grab each other's crotches
                and it's an all-male show,   the women
                    highly made-up
                        and strangely passive.

(i ask harold norse
    about marlon brando
        as we breakfast on eggs and coffee and jam that's too sweet.
            "He'd fuck anything that moves," harold replies,
                with a certain authority.   I wonder
about myself, and jeanne moreau . . . we could elope together
in the south of france and make movies . . . does patti smith spit
    every time she performs? . . . ntozake and her appetites—how
        we compare notes . . . would we really have
                        any children?)

Yolanda throws back her head and laughs, strutting defiantly
across the amsterdam stage. The stage
is littered with paper cups, hurled by the wild boys from the
balcony. She picks one up and throws it back
at a bewildered audience, the boys still writhing and delirious.
        "WHERE'S THE GLASS?" yolanda wants to know,
        "THE BROKEN SHARDS OF GLASS? WHERE ARE
        THE HALF-FINISHED BOTTLES OF BEER? DON'T THEY
        ALLOW THEM HERE?"

                She shows them her high-heeled boots
                    and flicks her tongue like a desert lizard.
"LORD . . . CAN YOU
        GET IT UP, JUST SO
            YOLANDA CAN SEE?"   She can't seem to stop laughing,
                                    shaking her long fingers
                                    like lacey fans:

        europe / europe / what
        a creature / all dis history /
        and no future . . .

84

The crowd becomes enraged,
pushing towards the stage. The young blond boys
climb up, running towards yolanda . . . she's standing still,
a half smile on her glistening ruby-red lips.
Yolanda sways in snakelike motion, holding the angry boys
at bay by some sort of musical hypnosis . . . her small, clear
voice singing:

> europe / europe / what
> a creature / all dis history /
> and no future . . .

The young boys remove their leather jackets and black t-shirts.
The band stops playing. IT'S YOLANDA'S SHOW, FINALLY—and she
motions for them to unzip their tight black pants.
>   (Some did it, mockingly. Some did it, cursing all
>   the while. Some did it, aggressively.
>   Some did it, with a certain surprising shyness.
>   But **they all did it**.)
Yolanda turns to the young girls in the audience, who seem
to be watching all this with a deep and mournful curiosity.
"**NOW LADIES**," yolanda says,
very slowly and deliberately, "**IS IT SEX,
OR IS IT DEATH**—or could there
be anything in between?"
>   She repeats this question several times, her voice
getting louder and louder. "**IS IT SEX, OR IS IT DEATH**—
or could there be anything
in between???"
>   "**Music!**" a young girl shouted.
>   "**Nothing!**" another one cried.
>   "**Metal!**" the women roared, mascara streaking
their pallid faces and mingling with a sudden flow of tears.
Even yolanda's eyes are wet, but she keeps grinning
as she looks at the waiting boys
some with hard-ons
some with semi hard-ons,
others without . . . their dicks
flaccid and pink,
like sleeping baby mice.
>   Yolanda orders the flaccid ones to drop to their knees and work on the
semi hard-ons with their mouths. The boys who are already erect begin
touching each other, enamored with each other's obvious virility.
>   Most didn't seem sure of their position. TO BEND OVER and be loved,
or to DO THE LOVING.

Some tried to touch and grab yolanda, who easily jumped out of their reach, gracefully avoiding the wild-eyed boys, dazzling the entire room with her intricate r & b choreography.

  "**TELL THE TRUTH TO YOURSELVES**," yolanda says
 to no one in particular. "**TELL THE TRUTH TO YOURSELVES,**
  and remember what your women have told you . . ."
With this, all
the women rose up in magnificent and beautiful fury,
screaming:

   "MUSIC!" "NOTHING!" "METAL!"

Yolanda disappeared into the night and caught the first available pan-am flight back to new york.

 I ran into her strolling down eighth street. Walking past me, she smiled and murmured in a sweet hoarse voice:

   "BLACK / BLACK . . . A JOB WELL DONE."

Ming The Merciless

dancing on the edge / of a razor blade
ming / king of the lionmen
sing / bring us to the planet
of no return . . .

king of the lionmen
come dancing in my tube
sing, ming, sing . . .
blink sloe-eyed phantasy
and touch me where
there's always hot water
in this house

o flying angel
o pteradactyl
your rocket glides
like a bullet

you are the asian nightmare
the yellow peril
the domino theory
the current fashion trend

ming, merciless ming,
come dancing in my tube
the silver edges of your cloak
slice through my skin
and king vulgar's cardboard wings
flap-flap in death
(for you)

o ming, merciless ming,
the silver edges of your cloak
cut hearts in two
the blood red dimensions
that trace american galaxies

you are the asian nightmare
the yellow peril

the domino theory
the current fashion trend

sing, ming, sing . . .
whistle the final notes
of your serialized abuse
cinema life
cinema death
cinema of ethnic prurient interest

o flying angel
o pteradactyl
your rocket glides
like a bullet
and touches me where
there's always hot water
in this house

Book Design by Jon Goodchild. Cover design by John Woo, with photograph by Steve Lovi.
Photograph of author by Don Nguyen. Etchings by Richard Powell.
Phototypeset in Italia Book by Sara Schrom,
at Type By Design, Fairfax, California.
Inside edit various by
Stephen Vincent, Gail Larrick
& Keith Abbott.